The Enemy's

THE ENEMY'S COUNTRY

Words, Contexture, and other
Circumstances of Language

GEOFFREY HILL

STANFORD UNIVERSITY PRESS
STANFORD, CALIFORNIA

Stanford University Press
Stanford, California
© 1991 Geoffrey Hill
Originating publisher: Oxford
  University Press, Oxford
First published in the U.S.A. by
  Stanford University Press, 1991
Printed in the United States of America
Cloth ISBN 0-8047-1903-9
Paper ISBN 0-8047-2368-0

Original printing 1991
Last figure below indicates year of this printing:
03 02 01 00 99 98 97 96 95 94

This book is printed on acid-free paper.

Deeds, it seems, may be Justified by Arbitrary Power, when words are question'd in a Poet.

DRYDEN

You cannot call a man an artist until he shows himself capable of reticence and of restraint, until he shows himself in some degree master of the forces which beat upon him.

POUND

PREFACE

THE text of this book is substantially that of the 1986 Clark Lectures, though 'Envoi (1919)' was extensively revised in 1987. I have also made a number of alterations, in both matter and style, to the first four chapters. Where appropriate the *Notes* are used to augment the discussion.

It is my pleasant duty to thank the Master and Fellows of Trinity College, Cambridge, for honouring me with their invitation to deliver the Lectures.

At various stages in its preparation the book has benefited from the close reading of Alice Goodman, Eric Griffiths, Donald Hall, Guy Lee, Richard Luckett, David and Katy Ricks, and John Waś. Their private comments have saved me from some public embarrassments. For all errors and infelicities that remain I am of course solely responsible.

I also gratefully acknowledge scholarly advice and practical assistance of various kinds from Robin Alston, Jonathan Barker, Peter Burke, Robert and Dorothy Gabe Coleman, William and Margaret Cookson, Yvonne Cripps, Brian Cummings, Alistair Elliot, Gerard Evans, Conor Gearty, Jeremy Hill, John Marenbon, Peter Rickard, Frank Stubbings, and Peter Walker.

It is both a pleasure and a sadness to recall here the name of a predecessor in the Lectureship, the late Humphry House, from whom I received, almost forty years ago, kindness and encouragement insufficiently acknowledged at the time.

Further debts are recorded among the *Notes*.

15 October 1990   G.H.

CONTENTS

A NOTE ON THE TITLE

I HAVE taken my title from Thomas Nashe and from William Davenant. In 'The Epistle Dedicatorie' of *Strange Newes*, an attack on the Cambridge pedant *G.H.*, Nashe commends the work to his 'verie friend' Apis lapis (Mr Beeston) with this flourish: 'Thou art a good fellow I know, and hadst rather spend ieasts than monie. Let it be the taske of thy best tearmes, to safeconduct this booke through the enemies countery.'[1] Davenant, in the 'Author's Preface' to *Gondibert*, has his conceit of 'the vast field of Learning, where the Learned . . . lye . . . malitiously in Ambush' and where one must 'travail . . .' as 'through the Enemy's country'.[2] Since I follow MacDiarmid in desiring 'a learned poetry wholly free | Of the brutal love of ignorance'[3] and hold, with John Berryman, that 'all the artists who have ever survived were intellectuals—sometimes intellectuals *also*, but intellectuals',[4] my choice of these sallies against learning may appear self-stultifyingly perverse. I will not stoop to the defensive innuendo that learning is antipathetic to 'true' intellect or that genius may be estimated by the depth of its immersion in 'meer Nature'. Nashe plïed his anti-pedantic learning with comic grace and Yeats's contrast[5] between young poets 'tossing' in lyric anguish and aged impotent scholars who 'edit and annotate' such gems of youthful suffering is a piece of sentimental cant. To 'think what other people think' is as likely to be the province of 'the popular boys'. If for 'vast field of

---

[1] *The Works of Thomas Nashe*, ed. R. B. McKerrow, reprinted with corrections and supplementary notes by F. P. Wilson, 5 vols. (Oxford, 1966), i. 258.
[2] *Sir William Davenant's Gondibert*, ed. D. F. Gladish (Oxford, 1971), 24.
[3] From 'The Kind of Poetry I Want', cited in *The Letters of Hugh MacDiarmid*, ed. A. Bold (London, 1984), 813.
[4] John Berryman, *The Freedom of the Poet* (New York, 1976), 215.
[5] In 'The Scholars': *The Collected Poems of W. B. Yeats*, 2nd edn. (London, 1950), 158.

A Note on the Title

Learning' we substitute 'vast apparatus of Opinion' we may be
nearer the mark. Intellect will always be learned, albeit at times
idiosyncratically. Of 'culture' and 'education' as currently
understood and practised, one feels less confident.
Davenant elected as his guide through the enemy's country
'his much honor'd friend M. Hobbes' as one who went 'not by
common Mapps' but 'painefully made [his] own Prospect'. My
book's subtitle is wrenched out of Hobbes. 'Words, contexture,
and other circumstances of Language'[1] I take to signify the
relation of word to word and of the body of words to those
contingencies and accommodations marginally glossed among
the 'Lawes of Nature' in *Leviathan*: 'covenants of mutuall trust',
'covenants extorted by feare', 'justice of manners and justice of
actions', 'submission to arbitrement', etc.[2]

[1] *Humane Nature* . . ., by Tho: Hobbes of Malmesbury (London, 1650), 51.
[2] Thomas Hobbes, *Leviathan*, ed. C. B. Macpherson (Harmondsworth, 1968), 196,
198, 207, 213.

A NOTE ON REFERENCES
IN THE TEXT

ALTHOUGH the bulk of the reference material is reserved to the last section of the book (pp. 105–41), I have, wherever practicable, given page-references immediately after quotations in the text. This has proved possible only in those cases where I have made recurrent reference to a particular volume or to a run of volumes. Citations within the text are as follows:

Chapter 1. *The Poems of John Dryden*, ed. James Kinsley, 4 vols. (Oxford, 1958); page-numbers run consecutively through the four volumes. *The Works of John Dryden*, ed. E. N. Hooker, H. T. Swedenberg, and others (Berkeley, 1956–); reference to this edition is by volume and page, e.g. '13: 49'. *The Letters of John Dryden*, ed. C. E. Ward (Durham, NC, 1942); references are prefaced by 'Ls'.

    Chapter 2. HUMANE NATURE: | Or, | The fundamental Elements | OF | POLICIE | . . . By THO. HOBBS of *Malmesbury*. | *London* . . . 1650; references to this edition are preceded by 'H'. OF | LIBERTIE. | AND | NECESSITY. | A TREATISE, | . . . By *Thomas Hobs*. | . . . LONDON, | . . . 1654; references preceded by 'L'. *Reliquiae Wottonianae* . . ., the editions of 1651 (A), 1654 (B), and 1672 (C). References to Dryden's letters and to the Oxford and Berkeley editions of his *Poems* and *Works* are indicated as in Chapter 1.

    Chapter 3. John Donne, *The Satires, Epigrams and verse Letters*, ed. W. Milgate (Oxford, 1967); reference by page-number. Izaac Walton, *The Compleat Angler 1653–1676*, ed. J. Bevan (Oxford, 1983); reference by page-number. I am reasonably confident that the context makes it clear whether the numbers refer to Donne or to Walton. References to *Reliquiae Wottonianae* as in Chapter 2.

A Note on References in the Text

Chapter 4. References for Dryden's poetry and prose are to the Oxford and Berkeley editions cited in Chapter 1.

Chapter 5. All notes and references will be found at the end of the book (pp. 132–41).

ONE

Unhappy Circumstances

AUBREY records that the philosopher Thomas Hobbes, although 'marvellous happy and ready in his replies' when baited by the 'witts at Court', was reluctant to 'conclude hastily' in questions of weight and import: 'he turned and winded and compounded in philosophy, politiques, etc. as if he had been at Analyticall worke.' This distinction between the particular virtues of instant repartee and of protracted and complex deliberation merits some remark at the present time when, it could fairly be said, the force of the distinction has been largely forgotten and when to 'turn' and 'wind' and 'compound' in one's arguments is to be taken as being contemptuously self-regarding, as holding oneself wilfully aloof from the proper business of discourse and communication.

When Hobbes defined his 'fifth Law of Nature' as 'compleasance', that is to say '*That every man strive to accommodate himselfe to the rest*', he established a mode of conduct and discourse for those who perhaps only partly understood him. Some twenty years after *Leviathan* appeared, an entire handbook, or 'conduct book' was devoted to *The Art of Compleasance or the Means to oblige in Conversation . . .*; and scholars of Restoration Comedy have shown how the 'double nature' of a society's dedication to ruthless self-gratification and to 'civility and affability' is accommodated in the word 'compleasance' itself. The very difficulty one has in defining the relationship between self-seeking and civility exemplifies the shifty utility of the term. It was observed of Mary Rich, Countess of Warwick, a good and charitable lady, that she was 'the foundress and

Notes, which are not cued in the text, are printed on pp. 105–41.

I

inventress, of a new science—the art of obliging', and it would be unjust to assume that her way of 'obliging' was equatable with the way 'to oblige in Conversation'.

One could perhaps say that self-gratification was sought and attained through the practice of civility or one could argue that 'patience, humility, civility and affability' were forms of humane reproof to the lust for selfish domination. In Etherege's *The Man of Mode* Harriet rebukes Dorimant: 'I am sorry my face does not please you as it is, but I shall not be complaisant and change it.' In Hobbes's terms she is playing at being '*Stubborn, Insociable, Froward, Intractable*' but as she acts out the frowardness she is all the more eloquently revealed as being beautiful, desirable, marvellous happy and ready in her replies. Beauty and status, in such theatre fictions, give every appearance of resolving the intractabilities of judgement and circumstance which the authors of those stage-fictions encountered not only outside the domain of the theatre but also within the contractual obligations and financial constraints of the business. Car Scroope's 'Prologue' and Dryden's 'Epilogue' to Etherege's play force the concept of 'Arbitrary Power' (178; cf. 1020) out of the charmed circle of the fiction, where it is taken care of in the spectacle of youthful and attractive ingenuity outwitting the twin tyrannies of crabbed age and commodity, into the immediate circumstances of the author's resentful dependence on a fickle and ignorant public which he mirrors to itself, aped and reflected in the least attractive humours and business of the stage. In Dryden's theatre prologues and epilogues the didactic satire of Jonsonian comedy and the bitter self-vindication of Jonson's 'An Ode. To himselfe' are compounded, though in the compounding a quite distinct timbre is realized. Jonson's 'Ode' proclaims the virtue of a 'high and aloofe' lyric *otium*. Dryden's most characteristic theatre work acknowledges that drudgery, *nec-otium*, is to be the medium of his achievement, its stultification and its paradoxical release. In this respect he is more 'Hobbesian' than is Rochester. The implications of '*That every man strive to accommodate himselfe to the rest*' are grained and cross-grained into the body of his work, as the incompatibilities of 'strive' and 'accommodate' are themselves wedged together in Hobbes's phrase. I would agree that, in the concluding moments of Etherege's play, Harriet's depiction of the 'great rambling lone house' of her rural exile has 'poignancy'; it is a brief but intensely memorable speech. 'Poignancy' will accommodate either pleasure or pain, rather as the heroine's own words move with elusive grace between ennui and *otium*. What she feels is ennui, or the prospect of it. Of the exquisite manner in which she diverts her sorrow one may say, as Dr Johnson said of one of Cowley's conceits, 'the mind must be thought sufficiently at ease' that can attend to the minute particulars of the fancy. Etherege's characters, even when unhappily circumstanced, retain an edge of advantage over the author of the 'Epilogue' who, at the time of the play's first performance in 1676, had recently incurred the enmity of the Earl of Rochester and who increasingly came to feel, in his dealings with the public world, the pressure of 'my unhappy Circumstances, that . . . have confin'd me to a narrow choice' (869).

These words were carefully rather than cautiously framed. The 'unhappy Circumstances' by 1697 were the social and economic consequences of his refusal to abjure the faith and practice of Roman Catholicism in the years following the abdication of James II. A member of a proscribed religion, Dryden was deprived of his public offices and had reason to anticipate difficulty in obtaining patronage. The 'Pastorals' were dedicated to the Roman Catholic nobleman Lord Clifford (869–73), the 'Georgics' in the same 1697 volume carried a dedication to the second Earl of Chesterfield (912–18), an adherent of the Stuart cause who had retired from public life when William of Orange took the throne. John Sheffield, third Earl of Mulgrave and Marquis of Normanby, 'Sharp judging *Adriel* the Muses friend' (239), to whom Dryden dedicated his translation of the *Aeneis* (1003 ff.) as well as the earlier *Aureng-Zebe*, was, though not a Catholic, a staunch supporter of the Duke of York, later James II. It is true that he managed his political accommodations with fair success under William III, but the exceptional constancy of his patronage, transcending political and religious factionalism, earned tributes not only from Dryden himself but also from John Dennis. As the judgement of these individual members of

3

the 'Learned Nobility' (869) resists and transforms unhappy circumstance so Dryden in his own more humiliating straits contrives a style which will give due emphasis to the sharpness of the affliction and to the fact that he is 'not dispirited with [his] Afflictions' (1424). To be narrowly confined is to be in straitened circumstances but to be confined to a narrow choice places the final emphasis on the limited freedom to choose. The word is not without spirit. Dryden can still contrive a touch of resonance from a flat recital.

The matter of how to relate *otium* to *negotium* (etymologically impacted, separable by means of paronomasia), the question of how to obtain, amid the world's circumstances, that 'vacation from other busines', the 'intervalls and ease' in which to think and write, are problems that have proved recurrently ponderable since Seneca composed his *De Brevitate Vitae* and *De Otio*. Francis Meres, in 1598, lamented the absence of any support for the 'famous and learned Lawreat masters of England' comparable to that which 'the Emperor Augustus, or Octauia his sister, or noble Mecaenas' lavished upon Virgil and Horace. Milton, keenly sensing how much he owed to his father's support, acknowledged the debt, both in the 'Ad Patrem' of *c.*1632 ('. . . Aeoniae iucunda per otia ripae . . .') and, ten years later, in *The Reason of Church-Government* ('Yet ease and leasure was given thee for thy retired thoughts out of the sweat of other men'). Dryden's letters and prefaces often revert to such matters, as do his 'Oxford' prologues and epilogues. John Locke refers to the problem in 'the Epistle to the Reader' introducing his *Essay Concerning Humane Understanding*, a work written, as he says, 'by incoherent parcels' and with 'long intervals of neglect'. The issues could not be more succinctly stated than they are by Ezra Pound in private letters and public tracts at the time of his attempt to raise funds sufficient to enable both Eliot and Joyce to devote their whole time and energy to writing: 'The only thing one can give an artist is leisure in which to work.' That was in 1922. Years later, in 1959, he added a footnote: 'Leisure is time plus money, or at any rate time without monetary worry.' As Dryden remarked in the last year of his life 'they who beare the purse will rule' (Ls 135). Dryden and Pound are indeed comparable in their awareness of the political and economic realities of circumstance, of the ways in which the writer's judgement of word-values both affects and is affected by his understanding of, or his failure to comprehend, the current reckonings of value in the society of his day. It is an irony to be briefly noted that Pound, unlike Eliot, was not an admirer of Dryden; he curtly dismissed the 'platitude and verbosity', 'that outstanding aridity'. Even so I would maintain that, judged by Pound's standard of measure ('you cannot call a man an artist until . . . he shows himself in some degree master of the forces which beat upon him'), Dryden's work manifests, albeit with varying degrees of finality, his command of the essential facts: that a poet's words and rhythms are not his utterance so much as his resistance. His 'choice of *Words*, and Harmony of Numbers' as Dryden would say, his 'technic' as Yeats and Pound called it, must resist the pressure of circumstances or be inundated by the tide of 'compleasance'. To the caveat that Pound's observation—an early one, from the *Patria Mia* of 1912—refers to a specific stage in a writer's development, the point at which the raw tiro becomes a genuine apprentice, a potential master capable of making his prize-song, I would respond that with every new work the true poet reverts to that condition. He cannot have a 'career' but as a lifelong apprentice-master he may well compose more than one masterpiece.

To suggest that Dryden accepted Hobbes's definition of value—'The *Value*, or WORTH of a man, is as of all other things, his Price', 'a mans Labour also, is a commodity exchangeable for benefit, as well as any other thing'—is to say only that he accepted it as an unhappy circumstance, especially in the case of his sometimes acrimonious dealings with Jacob Tonson, publisher in 1697 of *The Works of Virgil Translated into English Verse*. Dryden's value for the book-trade was equivalent to quantity of production and Tonson argued the price of the Ovid translations in a letter of 1692 accusing the poet of short-changing him: 'that makes for 40 guyneas . . . 1518 lines; And all that I have for fifty guyneas are but 1446' (Ls 51). Dryden in turn, in two letters of 1695, complained that Tonson had passed him base money: 'besides the clipd money, there were at least forty shillings brass'

(Ls 75). The state of the English currency at that time was 'deplorable'. There was a recoining of the silver money in 1696 but even this reformation left 'the poorer and more ignorant folk . . . with clipped money on their hands'.

It is not inappropriate that some of these contentious exchanges arose out of negotiations for the publishing of Dryden's *Virgil*. Dryden himself, I believe, is entirely aware of the poetic justice, the exemplary ironies, of labouring in his circumstances over the *Eclogues* and the *Georgics*. This latter work, particularly, is a sustained invocation to the virtues of '*labor*', hard work, the necessity for incessant vigilant toil in order to make Nature yield her richness. On the evidence of his own critical writings and autobiographical allusions it appears that Dryden bears in mind two kinds of '*labor*': the tenacity of the craftsman and the drudgery of the hack. It is a matter of angry pride with him to redeem the circumstances of the second by exercising the skill and judgement of the first. He suggests that in the *Eclogues*, an early work, Virgil's 'Pinions were not harden'd to maintain a long laborious flight' (870). His main criticism of Ovid is that 'as his Verse came easily, he wanted the toyl of Application to amend it' (795). The poet, like the rural craftsman, the husbandman, must expend time, knowledge, and effort in cutting back the over-luxuriant and in coaxing the stubbornly unproductive to yield. There is, however, a bleaker aspect to the Virgilian '*labor*', a harsher emphasis concentrated in the word '*improbus*' which is crucial to our understanding of the way Virgil has grasped the realities of agrarian circumstance. This is '*labor*' seen as a bare and bitter subsistence, 'endless Labour urg'd by need' (924) in Dryden's rendering, a phrase which even as he hit upon its clinching felicity must have struck home with infelicitous force of circumstance.

In his letters the word 'drudgery' is the one he most often applies, as if it were the wry appropriation of one of Shadwell's gibes (1919), to the circumstances of his working life: '. . . goeing to drudge for the winter' (Ls 13), 'my business heere is to unweary my selfe, after my studyes, not to drudge' (Ls 23), 'I am still drudging on: always a Poet, and never a good one' (Ls 109), 'I am still drudgeing at a Book of Miscellanyes' (Ls 113).

In Book XV of the *Metamorphoses*, a translation of which appeared in Dryden's last book, Ovid writes, in a passage devoted to sacrificial beasts, 'quid meruere boves, animal sine fraude dolisque, | innocuum, simplex, natum tolerare labores?' Dryden's version of these lines, 'How did the toiling Oxe his Death deserve, | A downright simple Drudge, and born to serve?' (1722), imbues the close rendering with a particular resonance. 'Downright' is the operative word, containing as it does the double sense of 'plainly' and 'merely'. Dryden contains in a clause that ambivalent feeling about innocence, guilelessness, which the word 'silly' also carried for a time; the suspicion that to be pious, holy, and good, in this world, is to be simpleminded.

His thinking is therefore complicated, in a way that directly affects the timbre of his style, by the fact that when he writes, as he not infrequently does, of his own 'labour' the word, basic as it sounds, has more than one connotation. It may mean a commissioned undertaking ('enjoin'd a fresh Labour' 1425) or it may connote those things which exhaust the mind and distract it from the tasks to which it is most suited ('when I labour'd under such Discouragements' 1424). It may also suggest, in Dryden as in Davenant, the 'Vigilance and labour' of one who must be constantly alert to those 'malitiously in Ambush', of one who 'travails through the Enemy's country'. Those are Davenant's phrases. Dryden writes of enemies too; the malice of the 'heavy gross-witted Fellows' (796) and their kind: 'What labour wou'd it cost them to put in a better Line, than the worst of those which they expunge in a True Poet?' (791-2). If in such emphasis on the inveterate hostilities both Davenant and Dryden may be called 'Hobbesian', that affinity depends less on paraphrasable philosophy than on tincture, 'as streams through Mines bear tincture of their Ore' (30).

There is evidence of such tincture in Dryden's version of the *Georgics*. The 'Ploughman' and 'the lab'ring Steer' (923) are downright English for 'hominumque boumque labores' but in 'lab'ring Husband' (927), 'lab'ring Swain' (928), 'lab'ring Hand' (929), 'lab'ring Hind' (931), Dryden is picking up from Virgil's text contingent implications, such as the 'durum genus' which

7

he translates as 'hard laborious Kind' (921), and is concentrating them in the English participle-adjective. Though not excluding all reference to 'sweet Vicissitudes of Rest and Toyl' that 'Make easy Labour' (921), Dryden places considerable emphasis upon the bare and bitter subsistence. Where Virgil writes that Winter, the farmer's lazy time, 'loosens the weight of care' ('hiems curasque resolvit') Dryden reworks it as 'Forget their Hardships, and recruit for more' (929). In the interpolated 'and recruit for more' genial relaxation becomes recuperation for yet 'more' hard labour; *otium* recharges the *negotium*; the remission is only a part of an unremitting pattern and Dryden labours to drive that irony home. In Virgil 'sightless moles dig out chambers' ('aut oculis capti fodere cubilia talpae'); in the English version 'the blind laborious Mole, | In winding Mazes works her hidden Hole' (925). The Latin 'fodere', 'to dig, or delve', is ponderously duplicated in the English by an adjective 'laborious' and by a verb 'works'.

It is exactly at this point, however, in the midst of this busyness, that we unearth a hidden oxymoron from the winding mazes of English poetry; for what Dryden's verse has idly discovered is that 'Mole' rhymes with 'Hole'. There is at times in the digging and delving of the craft a blind complicity between '*labor*' and '*otium*'. That which is 'laboured' may at the same time be 'otiose' for the 'laboured' may not, in fact, have been worked on enough. One may fairly ask of Dryden's 'lab'ring Husband', 'lab'ring Swain', 'lab'ring Hand', 'lab'ring Hind', and 'toiling Swain' (929) whether they are, after all, local intensifications of Virgil's counter-theme, '*labor*' as bare and bitter subsistence, or whether they are time-saving prefabrications that ease the verse along.

If this is indeed the case it demonstrates little more than that a major writer may be beset by the same minor problems which embarrass and confuse his lesser contemporaries. A minor problem left unmastered, however, comes to exercise a disproportionate advantage, and in the art of poetry it is so often the effortless that impedes. Mildmay Fane, second Earl of Westmorland, in his *Otia Sacra* of 1648, praises 'the virtues of contemplative quiet' and the withdrawal from the 'competitive *negotium'* of courtly and urban life. But even if his 'Rimes' are, as Fane says his were, 'beguilers of spare times', and even while he is propounding a doctrine of contemplative withdrawal, the poet is necessarily engaged in a competitive *negotium*; he is competing with the strengths and resistances and enticements of the English language. To fail to effect the essential negotiations with its fecund recalcitrance, its seeming complaisance, is to labour into otiosity ('Bidding me be of comfort, and not griev'd'; 'So should our frozen hearts be thaw'd, and Melt'; 'Thus then rows'd up and wak'ned, I began'; 'How's that attain'd? By heat, not cold'; 'Grant, with his Dayes, thy Grace increase, and fill | His Heart, nor leave there room to harbour ill'; 'But over-fed, we surfet'). When Dr Johnson wrote that in Cowley's poem on the death of Hervey there is 'a very just and ample delineation of such virtues as a studious privacy admits, and such intellectual excellence as a mind not yet called forth to action can display' the collocation of 'studious privacy' and 'not yet called forth to action' suggests that what he desiderates is an active involvement in the daily business of the world's affairs. As he wrote to the Reverend Dr Wetherell in 1776, 'Few things are more unpleasant than the transaction of business with men who are above knowing or caring what they have to do.' We need to make a clear distinction between this indictment of patronizing untroubled carelessness and the mood of 'frigid tranquility' with which, he claims, he dismisses his English Dictionary to the world; though a sense of the world's bland heedless power connects both statements. 'I have protracted my work till most of those whom I wished to please have sunk into the grave, and success and miscarriage are empty sounds'. Johnsonian sonority is here attuned to a hollow echo of itself and one cannot unperplex a philosophy of language from an aesthetic of style, an aesthetic of style from the unhappy circumstances.

It would be a just though simple abstract of such directly involved power to say that the *negotium* of language is inextricably a part of the world's business or that 'just as a man's language is an unerring index of his nature, so the actual strokes of his brush in writing or painting betray him and announce either the freedom and nobility of his soul or its meanness and limitation'. Mildmay Fane's sentiments, his philosophical programme, the paraphrasable content of his work, are above reproach; his brush-strokes are inept. One must therefore conclude that there is yet another oxymoron embedded in the inmost texture of English writing: the viciousness of virtue when virtue is not called forth to action in the *negotium* of language itself.

The example of the 'brush-stroke', which deeply influenced Ezra Pound's thinking, was suggested by Laurence Binyon, who had taken it from the ancient Chinese. The stress on the brush-stroke itself as the factive energy by which the 'subjective element', individual personality, is made one, for good or ill, with circumstance, contiguity, enables Pound to argue cogently for the ethical and aesthetic identity of the active intelligence and the public activity: 'the "statesman cannot govern, the scientist cannot participate his discoveries, men cannot agree on wise action without language", and all their deeds and conditions are affected by the defects or virtues of idiom'. I do not claim that in making this emphasis Pound has advanced beyond the position maintained by Samuel Johnson, who understood the clash and complicity between the self and circumstance and whose sardonic emphasis on 'above', in his indictment of those who engage in business while conceiving themselves superior to it, endorses his indignation that Gray in 'The Bard' was above knowing or caring about the actual mechanics of weaving a piece of cloth.

It is of course a matter of common observation that the actual mechanics of quotidian life, whether in the seventeenth or the twentieth century, are inevitably a matter of ambivalent regard. 'Business' has always been at once a necessary desirable activity furthering the proper concerns of the common weal and an arbitrary, tyrannical, distracting power preventing some other desirable activity or condition from reaching fulfilment. That such observations appear to gravitate so naturally to the oxymoronic is perhaps owing to an original Senecan artifice: the 'desidiosa occupatio' and 'iners negotium' of *De Brevitate Vitae*. The author of *Hudibras* wrote in his commonplace book

'Although the Management of almost all the Busnesse in the world may appeare very extravagant and Ridiculous, yet whosoever consider's it Rightly will finde that it cannot be avoyded, nor possibly be don any other way.' Butler's observation not only confronts an ambiguity, it also poses one. The question turns on what is meant by 'consider's it Rightly'. Does it imply 'with a shrewd appraisal of the going-rate of things' or 'according to justice and equity as in the old rightwiseness'? English poetry and prose, certainly since Chaucer, have registered many varied attempts to match the arts of language to the tough integument of 'Busnesse' by proposing various fictions in which the creative will can be imagined as operative above or below the middle ground of circumstance, the field of brokerage, negotiation, and compromise. The manner in which Andrew Marvell conceives of Cromwell as the '*Amphion*' of the English nation, 'Learning a Musique in the Region clear, | To tune this lower to that higher Sphere', or hymns the triumph of 'Choice' over 'Necessity' in Admiral Blake's victory over the Spaniards, is similar to the style in which Dryden celebrates the resistless genius of the newly dead, apotheosized Henry Purcell: 'Struck dumb they all admir'd the God-like Man' (863). 'Resistless genious' is Marvell's phrase; the panegyric to triumphant selfhood is common to both.

Students of seventeenth-century literature are told that when Dryden and his contemporaries speak of 'genius' they mean something less romantic than Coleridge's 'royal prerogative of genius' or Santayana's 'barbaric genius'; something more sober and reputable than 'Genius in the rôle of Caliban'. According to the usual caveats 'genius', to Dryden, would signify not the '*daimon*', not the 'strange and powerful *numen*' which, possessing the artist, marks him out as 'different and superior in kind', but a strong natural aptitude, the technical and temperamental affinity of the born craftsman for the raw materials of his *métier*. 'I find [Homer] a Poet more according to my Genius than Virgil' (Ls 121) is evidently temperamental affinity. 'Shakespear had a Genius for [Tragedy]' (Ls 71) just as evidently signifies a most forceful natural aptitude, as in 'A happy *Genius* is the gift of Nature.' But when Dryden observes that the 'distinguishing

Character' of Lucretius' 'Soul and Genius' is 'a certain kind of noble pride, and positive assertion of his Opinions' (395), this is something other than a matter of temperamental affinity, inherent gifts. 'He is every where confident of his own reason, and assuming an absolute command not only over his vulgar Reader, but even his Patron' (ibid). When Charles Blount writes to the Earl of Rochester 'No, my Lord, your mighty genius is a most sufficient argument of its own immortality', the implication 'different and superior in kind' is palpable. Rochester is being flattered by a social inferior as Dorset, Roscommon, Radcliffe, or Mulgrave are flattered by their social inferior Dryden and as the Earl of Pembroke is flattered by John Locke in the 'Epistle Dedicatory' to *An Essay Concerning Humane Understanding*. The historical accident that Rochester is a poet of great power does not annul the force of an original circumstance or of the expediency which it called forth into action. Dorset and Roscommon were mediocrities extravagantly praised by the professionals who depended on them. 'Genius' was evidently awarded *honoris causa* to men of high social standing, and low-born professionals were sometimes favoured by patrons for political reasons that had nothing to do with intrinsic merit. There are various shifts in the word 'genius' itself which suggest that it is 'combating betwixt two different Passions' as, in the essay *Of Dramatic Poesie*, the genius of Ovidian poetry is said to 'show the various movements of the soul' (17: 30). The root of the matter is perhaps to be found in Hobbes's distinction between natural and instrumental power. '*Naturall Power*, is the eminence of the Faculties of Body, or Mind: as extraordinary Strength, Forme, Prudence, Arts, Eloquence, Liberality, Nobility. *Instrumentall* are those Powers, which acquired by these, or by fortune, are means and Instruments to acquire more: as Riches, Reputation, Friends, and the secret working of God, which men call Good Luck.' The mixed feelings, then as now, about the nature and quality of 'genius' arise from the complex system of brokerage and bargaining between reciprocating groups of 'haves' and 'have-nots', a pattern discreetly sketched more than once in Dryden's letters to the aristocracy. The tone of seventeenth-century dedications strongly suggests that those

who possess 'instrumentall' power are to be credited with
'naturall' power as a perquisite of status ('the secret working of
God, which men call Good Luck') and that those who do not are
liable to find their 'naturall' power slighted or denied. When
Dryden depicts himself 'strugling with Wants, oppress'd with
Sickness, curb'd in my Genius, lyable to be misconstrued in all
I write' (1424), 'curb'd in my Genius' may mean 'when I
laboured under such discouragements at my honest trade of
versing' and it may also mean 'denied the true and just return
for my "naturall" power, my "extraordinary strength" of
"eloquence", through the "instrumentall" fiat of men of riches
and reputation'. Flattery of the patron is embedded in the same
stratum of speech and expectation as the self-justification of the
patronized.

 In writing as he did of 'naturall' and 'instrumentall' power
Hobbes codified certain perceptions about human nature and
conduct. He would not have claimed credit for initiating them.
The brief and fated equipoise, in Shakespeare's Richard III, of
natural and instrumental power is made manifest in the curt
swagger of '. . . whom I (some three monthes since) | Stab'd in
my angry mood, at Tewkesbury', the phrase indifferently
conceding superior self-knowledge and base self-exposure, the
preening *otium* of tyrannical power which will be forced to
acknowledge, by the end of the play, the pageant-like *negotium*
of traditional moral law in the procession of ghosts. There is
hierarchy even in this. In Marlowe's *Edward II* the professional
hanger-on Spencer says to his fellow practitioner Balduck 'You
must be proud, bold, pleasant, resolute, | And now and then
stab, as occasion serues.' 'Now and then stab' is a servile
popinjay version of a real tyrant's amoral *otium* of 'mood'. The
utterance of naked will, as much below the level of prescriptive
and proscriptive terms like 'moral' and 'immoral' as 'resistless
genious' is above the sordid brokerage of this world, is one that
haunts the 'just city', 'res publica', poets and philosophers—the
'Qual io fui vivo, tal son morto' of Capaneus or Richard of
Gloucester's 'I am my selfe alone', with which Dante and
Shakespeare dealt so comprehensively and comprehendingly.
The ambivalent power of 'What I was living, that am I dead' is

13

felt in Pound's 'E. P. Ode Pour L'Election de son Sepulchre' and in drafts of the 'Malatesta Cantos'. Pound translates Clytemnestra's words after the murder of Agamemnon as 'I did it. That's how it is.' We hear this pitch of voice in Mosca's cry in Canto XXVIII of the *Inferno*: 'Capo ha cosa fatta' ('A thing done makes an end'). In 1917 Pound claimed that the Renaissance enlightenment 'still gleams in the common Italian's "Così son io!" when asked for the cause of his acts'. Six years later he had modified his opinion: 'The Italian "*Così son io*," is a priceless heritage from the renaissance, but it is egocentric and possibly inferior to my grandmother's recognition of the demarcation and rights of personality'. The 'possibly' and 'my grandmother's' both concede and resist a worldly attitude to quaint old-fashioned scruple and certitude. Even if the energy declaring itself in 'That's how it is' or 'Capo ha cosa fatta' or 'Così son io' or 'Stone Dead hath no Fellow' or '*We have donne our businesse*' or 'stab as occasion serues' is conceived as being an irreducible monad of the assertive rebellious will, the judging imagination still persists in 'reducing' it, that is, 'bringing it into proper order', 'making it conformable or agreeable to a standard'. It is observable in this context that Dryden's lyric and discursive eloquence, in either of the two 'harmonies' of verse and prose, can be associated with that observation about Ovid: his capacity to 'show the various movements of a Soul combating betwixt two different Passions' (17: 30). Although it would be rash to attribute the opinions of a speaker in a dialogue to the author of that dialogue, these words of Eugenius may be applied to Dryden's own work. It is a characteristic traceable in the critical and polemical prose as well as in the reserved eloquence of 'To the Memory of Mr. Oldham'.

The suggestion that English poetry and prose, in the latter part of the seventeenth century, retained mass, density, gravity, that it did not reduce itself *instanter* to a compliance with those edicts about 'vicious abundance of *Phrase*', 'the ambitious obscurity of expressing more then is perfectly conceaved', is one that strikes less oddly on the scholarly ear today than it perhaps once did. Carew's admiring witness of achievement in the exemplary confrontation of genius with 'our stubborne language', as he phrased it in his elegy on Donne, persists in Davenant's conception of 'Poesy, which (like contracted *Essences* seemes the utmost strength and activity of Nature)'; and even Dryden's patron the Earl of Roscommon, in *An Essay on Translated Verse* (1684), esteems 'The comprehensive *English Energy* . . . | The weighty *Bullion* of *One Sterling Line*'. Dryden's acquaintance Richard Swan, a 'notorious punster', wrote, some time in the 1690s, a letter in an elaborately punning style, revelling in its own innocently vicious abundance of phrase, accusing the poet in wordy jest of not being a man of his word (Ls 137, 189). To go beyond such evidence, however, and to suggest that the 'stubborne language', the 'comprehensive *English Energy*', so thrives upon the unavoidable 'Busnesse' of the world as to become an equal *'daimon'* to that of 'genius' itself, a real 'strength and activity of Nature', is to hazard accusations of lexical mysticism. It is at such points, none the less, that we are bound to recognize the way in which the formal creative or critical judgement and the inchoate force of circumstance become awkwardly implicated or stand in irreducible confrontation. 'Meaning' itself either strives to accommodate, or strives to free itself from an accommodation which it feels as curb and compromise upon the integrity of utterance. One is reminded that the 'vultum clausum' attributed by Clarendon to Henry Vane the Younger and the *'viso sciolto'* recommended by 'an old Roman courtier' to Sir Henry Wotton, and by Wotton to the young John Milton, although seemingly antithetical, are alternative masks for venturing into the world of 'Busnesse', where the different shades of meaning tend to pass into or include each other. They are formal expressions of the same essential policy, for being as Izaac Walton put it 'as free and open-hearted, as discretion will warrant me to be with a stranger' or, as Marvell reportedly put it more bluntly: 'not play[ing] the good-fellow in any man's company in whose hands he would not trust his life'.

The more gifted the writer the more alert he is to the gifts, the things given or given up, the *données*, of language itself. Conversely, the otiosity and vacuity of formal language occur when the writer's energy of judgement is not equal to the force of circumstance, to the strength and activity or to the resistant inertia of 'our stubborne language'. The writer may be simply inept or he may fancy himself above the gravitational field of the *negotium*; or he may feel under some contractual or other obligation to descant fancifully upon a suggestion that he knows to be in fact a gross yet tenuous hyperbole. The fatuous poetry and prose of the late seventeenth century are often fatuous because of their readiness to oblige. 'To be admitted your *Menial* is, in effect, a Maintainance for Life: And what may the good Servant expect when even the bad (such as my self) meet with Rewards so unproportion'd to any Merit they can pretend by their Service.' Even as Robert Gould balances his clauses he recognizes that what he is about is unbalanced, 'unproportion'd'. His poems, indeed, show some bitterness towards the '*Quality*', 'the Fools of *Title* and *Estate*'. A seemingly infinite obligingness of language may indicate an onerous burden of obligation, though the obligation may be only that of accommodating oneself to expectation. The work of Gould's friend John Oldham was immortalized by Dryden as 'harsh' and 'rugged' (389) but those epithets are themselves under some constraint, judiciously poising the alternatives of censure and praise. Oldham laboured to achieve decorum and smoothness, succeeding well enough for Ezra Pound, in the *ABC of Reading*, to praise the 'sustained' 'melody' of his elegy on Rochester, the translation of the *Epitaphios Bionos*. And Oldham's faults, elsewhere in his work, were as much those of vacuity and otiosity as of roughness or lameness. His praise of 'holy Prodigality' is itself prodigal of fancy, and when he likens his subject to the 'All-great Creator, who | Can only by diffusing greater grow' he is both effusive and diffuse. A line such as 'The boundless Stock can never be exhausted quite' shows all too clearly how bounded and exhausted the invention is. This is language addressing itself to the topic as Gould addresses himself to the Earl of Abingdon; it finds itself situated like the 'Poor' in Dryden's 'Eleanora' (his elegy for Abingdon's wife), who have become accustomed to take her wondrous bounty for granted: 'So sure the Dole, so ready at their call, | They stood prepar'd to see the Manna fall' (586). 'Prepar'd' here means 'in a posture to receive' and it also means complacent in expectation. To be so 'prepar'd' is to be ill prepared, redeless. When 'inspiration', which Davenant fairly calls 'a dangerous word' and which Hobbes likens to the workings of a 'Bagpipe', is taken, as it commonly is, to mean going along with the prevailing windy cant, with whatever currently passes for divine *afflatus*, it becomes indistinguishable from the tamest *bienséance*. 'Poetique Rage' is reduced to a convenient tag rhyming with 'frantick Age', 'guilty Age', and so on. The manna of inspiration is nothing more than an inspired manner.

Dryden himself is by no means free from tags, such as the easily 'shining Share' (927) where Virgil has the 'durum . . . dentem', the 'hard tooth' of the 'blunted share'. 'Eleanora', a commissioned elegy for a woman 'whom he had never seen', endeavours to 'fix' 'Virtue's Image' in imitation of Eleanora's own resolute qualities and to stress 'th' Impressions of her Mind' (591) by the particularly emphatic return upon this rhyme-word ('so large a Mind', 'rare Endowments of the Mind', 'glimpses of her glorious Mind' 591–2). Such routine offerings as 'Look on thy tender Pledges left behind' or 'And shed a beam of Comfort from above' (594) or 'One sigh, did her eternal Bliss assure' (593) are the merest 'bye-writing' of panegyric. However, when Keats employed this term, perhaps by analogy with 'by-talk', he was remarking how, in *King Lear*, Shakespeare can transform the routine, the commonplace, the 'uninspired', into something 'more marvellous than the whole ripped up contents of Pernambuca'. In 'They stood prepar'd to see the Manna fall' Dryden meets their idle expectation that it always will with his knowledge that in due course their servile complacency will be disappointed. Charity has its laudable place, as has laudatory verse; at the same time this language takes the measure of those common vices which habitually tag themselves to uncommon virtue.

Dryden is able to involve, to creative ends, the stubborn linguistic strength and complaisant activity of the English tongue with the wilfulness and ignorance of the English people, the crowd's 'gross instinct, of what pleases or displeases them' (13: 13). 'For, we are fallen into an Age of Illiterate, Censorious, and Detracting people.' So Dryden wrote in the essay prefixed to *The State of Innocence, and Fall of Man . . .*, his 'tagged' version of *Paradise Lost*. 'For, we are fallen' carries a sense both of fortuitous occurrence and of guilty consequence: 'it is our chance misfortune to be so circumstanced' or, 'inveterate depravity wills that it shall be so'. Doctrinal theology has here reduced itself to a more accommodating turn of phrase but there is no simple distinction between Hobbesian secularism and Miltonic theology. As might be expected of those whose 'Interests and Tenets did run counter to each other', Hobbes and Milton have created complementary worlds; and insofar as Dryden is working a Hobbesian vein he is to a correlative extent Miltonic. The stratum of deliberation into which, and out of which, he works with his most characteristic energy is one which the author of *Paradise Lost* would have regarded as theologically and ethically dubious: I mean that rich and dangerous vein of proud, resentful, yet stoical consciousness of injured merit which provides a distinctive tincture in the 'Preface' to *All for Love*, the epistle to Sir Godfrey Kneller, numerous theatre prologues and epilogues, and in the 'Postscript' to the translation of *Virgil's Aeneis* ('curb'd in my Genius . . . not dispirited with my Afflictions' 1424). The tone here approaches that which in Milton is the expression of the archetypal rebellious will. It is equally the case that Dryden places a strong emphasis upon the virtue of the 'Legislative style' ('Plain and Natural, and yet Majestick . . . A Man is to be cheated into Passion, but to be reason'd into Truth' 311). The legislative style is Dryden's equivalent to the Seraph Abdiel.

It is therefore all the more worthy of remark that so much of his distinctive energy springs from his openness to 'passion', understood both as the effect of cheating eloquence and as the source of 'noble eagerness' (13: 38):

> How I lov'd
> Witness ye Dayes and Nights, and all your hours,
> That Danc'd away with Down upon your Feet,
> As all your bus'ness were to count my passion.

(13: 49)

The power of these words stems from the fact that they simultaneously excite and appease contradictory forces of emotions, powers which, brought into such contact, ought to be self-stultifying but which, mysteriously, we feel, are not. Antony has a genius for love and a genius for being fated, and his words illuminate the 'secret working of God, which men call Good Luck' in more than one way. They have something of the dolphin-like bounty and largess of genius and something of the arrogance of privileged *otium* that can so make a hyperbole of itself, as though in taking liberties with rhetoric one were actually making oneself free of fate. This speech is the summation of the bitter reproach heaped upon Antony by his own remorse and by the indignation of his devoted followers, accusations of 'desperate sloth' (13: 35) and 'inglorious ease' (13: 33), but it is also crossed with a weft which maintains that Cleopatra's remembrance of 'transcendent passion' (13: 40) is equally true. It is both retrospective and prescient. Gathering up all that can be said by way of recrimination it yet anticipates the Hobbesian apotheosis of the lovers in which culpable lust is transfigured as a lustre appropriate to 'Princes, and men of conspicuous power (anciently called *Heroes*)'. For Dryden, the maker and arbiter of Antony's eloquence, the 'conspicuous power' manifests itself in the magisterial trope 'As all your bus'ness were to count my passion' in which the 'bus'ness of the World' (13: 49), 'the bus'ness of Mankind to part us' (13: 48), has its narrow moral triumph snatched away into the power of its beleaguered adversary. The destructive business of time, attrition, misjudgement, folly, the vacuous, otiose hyperbole of bad Restoration 'heroique', all the 'unhappy circumstances' of life and art, turned at one stroke of defiant judgement into infinite leisure!

TWO

The Tartar's Bow and the Bow of Ulysses

'TUNEFUL and well measur'd Song', as Milton praised it in his tribute to Henry Lawes's word-setting, is not exclusively a matter of technique. It also involves a recognition and acceptance of one's place in the scheme of things. The musician, spanning words 'with just note and accent', shows his mastery in acknowledging that the poet is master. It is the composer's duty and privilege to 'humor' the English tongue, to 'comply with [its] peculiar nature and exigencies' and perhaps to confer, by so doing, 'a particular character or style'. The distinction between advocating technical compliance and maintaining the civil 'Arts of Complacency and good behaviour' (645) is not always easily drawn; and our literature might be less rich and resonant if things were otherwise. Milton's sonnet pays its own tribute to reciprocity, and not merely in a phrase or two of stately cant ('Thou honour'st Verse, and Verse must lend her wing | To honour thee, the Priest of *Phoebus* Quire'). The poem did not achieve its final form without trial and error and is, even now, not impeccable. Against the exemplary handling of enjambment, 'span | Words', where the phrasing does what it says, reaching across the bar-line to place its 'Words' on the right spot with just the right emphasis, one has to set an infelicity in the matching of lines two and three ('how to span . . . not to scan . . .'). It is not the rhyme itself that produces this effect but the syntax: the little jingle of 'how to . . . not to'. Milton's drafts show him worrying at his phrasing, here and elsewhere in the sonnet. In line three he first wrote 'words with just notes, wch till then usd to scan' and then tried 'when most were wont to

21

scan'. In line eight he changed 'that didst reform thy art, the cheif among' to 'That with smooth aire couldst humor best our tongue'. One senses that Milton, in 1646, is a little troubled by a matter that has continued to vex musical scholarship: the question of how far the claim that Lawes 'first taught' the 'declamatory' *stilo recitativo* to English song-writers is fair to his contemporaries. Lawes himself, in words that closely resemble Milton's, said that it was John Wilson who 'taught . . . our Language, first, to speak in Tone'. Modern scholarship cites the names of Coperario and Lanier, and one is reminded that Ferrabosco had experimented with recitative. But equally good authority holds that Milton's praise is not excessive, that Lawes was the first to practise the art with consistent excellence, and that the sonnet intends no more than this.

Notwithstanding such caveats it seems fair to say that, as he drafted, Milton could scarcely avoid pondering, phrase by phrase, the nature of truthfulness and equity and the possibility that, in a sonnet praising proportion, his praise might be disproportionate. The little vacuity of 'how to . . . not to' creeps in as the more perplexedly judicious 'wch till then us'd to' and 'when most were wont to' are successively eased out. Milton is also 'humoring' several 'exigencies'; he too is composing a 'smooth aire', yet the smoothness is affected by a perplexity which, even as it is being erased, leaves its mark on the syntax of the *textus receptus*.

It does not seem to me that, in making this emphasis, one is unduly imposing one's own perplexities. Thomas Hobbes stated, in his treatise of *Humane Nature*, that 'there is scarce any word that is not made *equivocal* by divers contextures of speech, or by diversity of pronunciation and gesture' (H 50–1). Milton's sonnet is a 'gesture' that takes as its topos 'diversity of pronunciation' ('Words with just note and accent', 'committing short and long'). Nor is it wholly without equivocation. It is not absolutely invulnerable to Hobbes's charge that '*Ratio* now is but *Oratio*' (H 56). It will be objected that Hobbes, like Bacon, regarded equivocation, all forms of ambiguity in language, as 'intolerable' and worked for their eradication; and, from that, it may be concluded that he and Bacon were at liberty to stand aloof from the 'intolerable wrestle | With words and meanings'. Empirical observation confirms that this is not so. Bacon, in *The Advancement of Learning*, argues that 'wordes, as a *Tartars* Bowe, doe shoote backe vppon the vnderstanding of the wisest, and mightily entangle, and peruert the Iudgement'. He is not offering an aloof analysis for, as he says, 'it is not possible to diuorce our selues from these fallacies and false appearances, because they are inseparable from our Nature and Condition of life'. His thesis moves forward in the direction of 'the wisedome of the *Mathematicians*' and the 'definitions of our wordes and termes' but his gaze is also retrospective, looking towards Plato's 'fayned supposition . . . of the Caue' ('our spirites are included in the Caues of our owne complexions and Customes'). It may be a 'fayned supposition', but the inseparability of 'fallacies and false appearances' from our progressive endeavours is not treated as a mere *'fiction* of the Minde' (H 24). Bacon may be compromising with an equivocation (Hobbes would say that 'all *metaphors* are by profession *equivocal*' H 50) but that is a different matter. In translating this passage into Latin Bacon found himself engaged upon the clearance of his own meaning. Where he had originally seemed to suggest that the defining of our words precludes confusion of judgement he now inserted 'attamen haec omnia non sufficiunt' and his analogy of the Tartar bowman reads more cogently here than in the original English: '. . . retro in intellectum (unde profecta sint) retorqueant.'

Meaning, for Hobbes, is implicated with intent. For example, 'it is *necessary* . . . to *trace* and *finde out*, by many Experiences, what men do mean by calling things just and unjust' (H 41). 'What men do mean . . .' stands here both for the sense in which we are to take men's words and for the sense which they contrive to impose upon their words. When we ask of someone 'What do you mean by it?' we are not implying that a literal translation will suffice. We are objecting to an imposition, to an intent that we suspect we discern; we are letting it be known that we wish to trace and find out the whole *'drift,* and *occasion,* and *contexture* of the speech, as well as the *words* themselves' (H 51). The use of names is 'imposed arbitrarily by men' (H 40) partly through politic deliberation, partly because such impositions are 'inseparable from our Nature and Condition of life' and because, as Hobbes says, '*Deliberation* is nothing else but . . . alternate *hope* and *fear*' (L 68). Thus, in arguing that we must find out by experience 'what men do mean', he himself compounds with an equivocation, not in order to evade a question but to intensify the sense of a necessary perplexity ('*free from Necessitation* I say, no man can be' L 45).

If what a writer 'means' is what he advocates, or may be supposed to advocate, his 'thesis' or programme, Hobbes's meaning is not unrecognizable in that 'collective body of assumptions' which the minor literature of an age makes current. Sir Robert Howard's notion, resolutely challenged by Dryden, that in questions of aesthetic judgement one cannot 'infringe the Liberty of Opinion' or 'censure the satisfaction of others' and that the author's, or spectator's 'taste', that is to say his unregulated fancy and prejudice, is the sole and rightful arbiter, may possibly derive from Hobbes's observation that 'the *Smell* and *Taste* of the *same thing*, are *not* the *same* to *every man*, and therefore are *not* in the thing *smelt* or *tasted*, but in the *men*' (H 17). Howard's complaisant assumption is merely another idol of the market-place. Hobbes wrote that 'by *Spontanity* is meant *inconsiderate action*' (L 74); he also said that a thing may be 'easie and plain . . . but withal false' (L 46).

Hobbes's 'meaning', therefore, comprises an argument, a thesis which is unequivocal, which looks 'providently towards the future', and a counter-argument, realized within the texture of his writing, which grasps that the equivocal and the ambiguous are intrinsic to human nature and civic history. One is so impeded by custom, opinion, circumstance, and all other forms of 'tyrannizing' (L 50), by appetite, passion, a density of 'inconsiderate action', 'too *hasty* concluding' (H 2), 'the rash embracing of wrong principles' (L 35), 'hard sayings' (L 64), that 'the *contrary* must needs appear a great Paradox' (H 8). 'Paradox' is itself 'intrinsecal' to Hobbes's work and coexists with a didactic incisiveness which would be glad to see it erased from human discourse. On the one hand 'Colour is not inherent in the Object, but an effect thereof upon us' (H 16); on the other, there are impediments which are 'intrinsecal', 'in the nature' of things (L 70). '*Liberty*', he writes, '*is the absence of all the impediments to Action that are not contained in the nature and intrinsecal qualitie of the Agent*' (L 69–70). This return upon the 'intrinsecal' from the non-inherent is one of several epitomes of stylistic method that may be perilously abstracted from the texture of his work. Intrinsic quality of style is the simultaneous recognition of strength and impediment which, as it declares itself triumphantly possessed of such knowledge, suffers the ignominious consequences of that possession. Even the most unequivocal utterance is affected by the circumstantial and contingent matter implicated in our discourse, 'which being derived from the custom and common use of speech, representeth unto us not our own conceptions' (H 51). As with his contemporaries, Hobbes's word both for the continuity or contiguity of things and for the structure and composition of artefacts is 'contexture'. One might, in the seventeenth century, have 'certain fortuitous Concretions and Contextures of Atoms', 'a regular Contexture of continued Policy', and 'The Contexture of sentence with sentence'. When Hobbes writes that 'we are to consider the *drift*, and *occasion*, and *contexture* of the speech, as well as the *words* themselves', it is 'drift' and 'contexture' that tune the sentence. 'Contexture' here is close to 'circumstance' understood as 'the totality of surrounding things'. In the next sentence he adds 'It is therefore a great ability in a man, out of the words, contexture, and other circumstances of Language, to deliver himself from *Equivocation*, and to finde out the true meaning of what is said' (H 51). Here the 'words' precede and partly subsume the 'contexture', and the 'circumstances' appear less as 'the totality of surrounding things' than as the 'material adjuncts', the 'things belonging' to language. Extrinsic and intrinsic 'contexture' are related but the nature and extent of that relationship are indeterminate. We may feel that such implications are largely substantiated by our experience, our understanding, but they remain implications, gathered from 'the Contexture of sentence with sentence'. We are uncertain whether the body of a text is a real embodiment or merely the idea of one. Our most effective words which, Puttenham says, 'make yeelding and flexible' 'the minde of man' encounter in Hobbes a 'necessitie' against which they are of 'no effect' (L 55). Language, even as it takes the measure of things, falls short. Its various formalities, syntax, prosody, etc., are enacted partly within the domain of a paradox: that its limitations and inadequacies are defined by its own cogency and eloquence; but there remain circumstances which baffle all attempts at definition. Poetic measure (metre and cadence), like other adjuncts of 'Oratio', is a manifestation of 'Custom' which 'hath so great a power, that the Minde suggesteth onely the first word; the rest follow *habitually*' (H 56) while, at the same time, it is the power to override, with its ever-renewing capacity for springing and counterpointing, the habitual and the customary.

It would be an absurdity, however, to suggest that English writers required the sanction of Bacon and Hobbes before engaging with these intrinsic perplexities. When Chaucer employs the identical line 'Allone, withouten any compaignye', once, in 'The Knight's Tale', in a plangent threnody, and once, soon afterwards, in 'The Miller's Tale', describing the 'chambre' of 'hende Nicholas', he shows himself not unaware of the necessity for considering 'the *drift*, and *occasion*, and *contexture* of the speech, as well as the *words* themselves'. The measures of Skelton and Wyatt anticipate the perception that 'our discourse . . . being derived from the custom and common use of speech, representeth unto us not our own conceptions'.

'Measure' in *The Arte of English Poesie* 'is but the quantitie of a verse, either long or short'. In Skelton's *Magnyfycence* 'Measure' is a moral idea ranged against the 'wylde Insolence' of 'Lyberte': 'I ponder by nomber; by Measure all thynge is wrought'. 'Nomber' here signifies order and aggregation in all their forms, but the particular sense of 'conformity, in verse or music, to a certain regular beat or measure' was also current at that time. Skelton, in *Magnyfycence*, makes his metrical variations, from rime royal to macaronic hexameter or to the so-called tumbling verse, embody and enact his ethical priorities. It is a commonplace to say that the play is deficient in 'character-drawing'. This is to overlook the evidence that in such passages as the soliloquy of Clokyd Colusyon, who employs, because he is a courtly hypocrite, the magisterial Chaucerian rime royal already adopted by Measure and Felycyte, the character is in the measure:

> To passe the tyme and order whyle a man may talke
> Of one thynge and other to occupy the place,
> Then for the season that I here shall walke,
> As good to be occupyed as vp and downe to trace
> And do nothynge; how be it, full lytell grace
> There cometh and groweth of my comynge;
> For Clokyd Colusyon is a perylous thynge.

'Measure' here is both the gravity of the form and Clokyd Colusyon's taking its measure with perverse and meditative relish. He takes the measure of his situation physically ('*Hic deambulat*') and metaphysically ('And craftely can I grope howe euery man is mynded'). This recital of his own motives and actions is simultaneously an enactment of the ways in which such evil genius is disseminated among mankind. Idle people desire to be entertained; Clokyd Colusyon is entertaining them. *Magnyfycence* is an entertainment, 'A goodly interlude and a merry'. Clokyd Colusyon is rightly estimating his place in the world's business; that is his *métier*; but Skelton is also considering him rightly, according to the measure of righteousness. The rectitude of such verse is manifested in its capacity to measure up to the demands of active vice and to the authority of active virtue; it is a brooding third force in which the magisterial rime royal and the cynical travesty of the magisterial style are balanced but not equated.

Wyatt's 'They fle from me that sometyme did me seke' is at one with, while it is at odds with, the aristocratic Chaucerian idioms, like those in 'The Squire's Tale'. The formalities of Wyatt's poem are reminiscent of the courtly love-complaint of an earlier generation; its intimate procedures are not. '[H]er armes long & small' sounds like Charles d'Orleans; 'meke', 'fortune', 'gentilnes', 'new fangilnes' all have a Chaucerian tincture. But though intensely evocative of older styles of conduct and expectation, 'gentil', 'gentilnes', are still part of Wyatt's own speech and have not been artificially resurrected. '[G]ood and gentill fashons', 'gentill wordes and fashon', 'gentill and good answer', are phrases found in his diplomatic correspondence. 'And I have leve to goo of her goodenes' is a barbed variant of such 'good and gentill fashons'. As a diplomat, and an author of careful dispatches, he was well placed to observe and assess occasions of disadvantage, ill-suitedness, and perilous 'variance'; and it is variance with which 'They fle from me' is engaged. The strength of a word like 'gentil' is also its weakness; its weakness is its strength. 'Good and gentill fashons' are powerful enough to be called upon, even by those who have no intention of acting upon the principles which sustain them. They are derided, yet they defy derision:

> It was no dreme I lay brode waking
> > but all is torned thorough my gentilnes
> > into a straunge fasshion of forsaking
> > and I have leve to goo of her goodenes
> > and she also to vse new fangilnes
> > but syns that I so kyndely ame serued
> I would fain knowe what she hath deserued

Chaucer himself precludes our saying that Wyatt's poem takes to the point of parody the irrelevance of 'Chaucerian' courtly values at the Court of Henry VIII or in the various diplomatic milieux of Europe. The inherent contradiction in 'gentilnesse', 'curteisie', is that, while being adjuncts of worldly privilege and spiritual authority, they are susceptible to parody and worse forms of insult, rendering their possessors liable to humiliation and servitude. Chaucer knew this. So, for that matter, did the author of *The Ancrene Riwle*, who instructed his gentle-born anchoresses to offer up as a form of penitential oblation their endurance of 'haughty behaviour at the hands of those who might once have been [their] serfs'. Curteisie may be no more than nervous over-refinement expressing itself in unwitting self-parody. On the other hand some forms of affronted fastidiousness may appear naïve and comical only when viewed from a prejudiced standpoint which is itself nothing but a mode, which Chaucer and Wyatt both call 'newfangleness'. But if it is true that Wyatt consolidates Chaucer's findings it is also true that he fragments Chaucer's certitudes. In Arcite's death-speech in 'The Knight's Tale' there is an atonement between sexuality and *gentilesse*. Wyatt's inventiveness in 'They fle from me' is shown in the way he stresses the divisiveness, the division between them. He has, however, charged his verse with the task of rendering even this accountable. He has embodied the abruptness, astonishment, flat dejection, in the pace and pause of the line: 'But syns that I so kyndely ame serued | I would fain knowe what she hath deserued'. Accountability is rendered through paronomasia.

Paronomasia, according to Henry Peacham in *The Garden of Eloquence*, is 'a figure which declineth into a contrarie by a likelihood of letters, either added, changed, or taken away'. Puttenham writes of 'prosonomasia' whereby words 'do pleasantly encounter and (as it were) mock one another by their much resemblance', as in 'proue' and 'reproue'. Wyatt's 'kyndely' tacitly declines into a contrary as the ingenuous compiler of *Tottel's Miscellany* conceded and confirmed in changing it to 'vnkyndly'. 'Serued' and 'deserued' encounter and mock one another by their much resemblance, but not 'pleasantly'. The seventh chapter of the third book ('Of Ornament') of *The Arte of English Poesie* reveals that its author, perhaps more than some other Elizabethan instructors in eloquence, gave attention to those figures which 'passe the ordinary limits of common vtterance', drawing the mind 'from plainnesse and simplicitie to a certaine doublenesse', but it also reveals that, for him, 'keeping measure' was pre-eminently 'pleasant conueyance', the poet being 'appointed not for a iudge, but rather for a pleader, and that of pleasant & louely causes and nothing perillous, such as be those for the triall of life, limme, or liuelyhood'. Puttenham's chapter is itself a 'figuratiue speach', a mild form of 'merry skoffe', ensuring that, after all, figures which pass the ordinary limits of common utterance do not pass the ordinary limits of proper amusement provided for 'princely dames, yong ladies, gentlewomen and courtiers' in Elizabethan England.

One is not arguing, either ingenuously or disingenuously, that a mountebank spontaneity of self-expression should usurp the role of studied 'ornament poeticall'. There remains, none the less, a proximity between Wyatt's 'kyndely' and Puttenham's 'pleasantly' that is also 'the spacious bredth of [a] diuision'. In the 'Defence' prepared by Wyatt for his trial in 1541 one finds a figure precisely anticipating one of Puttenham's examples of prosonomasia: 'proue and reproue.' Wyatt writes 'I doute not but the reste of there proffes wilbe but reproffes in euerie honeste mans iudgmente'. For Wyatt, in these circumstances, the matter of 'but one smale syllable chaynged' is not a 'prety' optional embellishment but the nub of his predicament. '[W]hat thynge is that that these mene wolde not wreste for there purpose that wreste suche thynges?' One is not arguing, either, for the status of 'circumstance' as an arbiter or for the moral superiority of some notional 'experience of real life' over the unrealities of bookish rhetoric. Puttenham himself, faced with certain charges in 1570, poised his defence on the precise interpretation of the word 'goodnesse' and in another work attributed to him, the *Justificacion*, a defence of Elizabeth's policy in 'the Affaire of Mary Queene of Scottes', he shows some casuistical skill in the choice and interpretation of words. The question is not one of quantitative differential in 'real and substantial action and suffering' nor of the supposed marginal status of 'ornament poeticall', 'figures rhethoricall', in the 'practisis' and 'trafiques' of the world. The question is rather one of a qualitative difference in realization. Wyatt, in his 'Defence', masters his fear and focuses his indignation through bookish rhetoric, not in spite of it. One's case for the outstanding merit of 'They fle from me' is based on the recognition that some writers, more than others, realize (understand and establish as contextual fact) that the 'figures' do not run in pleasant and lovely parallel to 'practisis' and 'trafiques' but are inextricably a part of the world's figuring and trafficking, and that this is a circumstance which the 'figures' are bound at once to suffer and to judge. Donne's Verse Letters to Sir Henry Wotton or Nashe's *Pierce Penilesse His Svpplication to the Diuell* are metaphysical in the way that Troilus's speech on the defection of Cressida is metaphysical: in the realization that their conceits, however strained, are less fantastic than the common effects of custom and habit and the everyday 'wrestings' of accident or of deliberate cruelty and malice. Wotton, when he died in 1639, left this 'prudent, pious Sentence' (as his biographer Walton calls it) to be placed on his tombstone: 'DISPUTANDI PRURITUS FIT ECCLESIARUM SCABIES . . . THE ITCH OF DISPUTATION WIL PROVE THE SCAB OF THE CHURCH' (A c8ᵛ). There is a place for such 'morall Images, and Examples' and Puttenham's knack, much admired by his modern editors, of demonstrating how 'the "fleering frumpe" is accompanied by "drawing the lippe awry, or shrinking vp the nose" ' does not in itself constitute a superior form of observation. It is Nashe who, in 1592, wrests out of rhetoric, common speech, and common observation a style in which the 'fain[ing]' of 'Poets' both judges and· is judged by the feigning of those who are not 'poets'. 'Ovt vpon it, how long is Pride a dressing her selfe?' is as clear to the eye as is Puttenham's 'fleering frumpe'; more than that, it enlivens sententiousness with a pretty pun to make an oblique judgement on rhetorical style itself. Nashe is presciently translating Wotton's 'pruritus' and 'scabies' from axiom into activity. His writing closely ruminates upon the world's itch, its unending contumacious prurience, and the recurrent exclamations of his style involve the angry cries of the bewildered people with his own 'iesting' anger that things are so. In such writing we are at least given some ground for suggesting that words, even when they 'bend' or 'twist back' upon the progress of the argument, are not bound to do so destructively, as Bacon's figure of the Tartar bowman would suggest; it is not inevitable that words rebel against all attempts at better distinction, even when rebellion and loss of distinction are the matter of their contemplation.

It could be argued that in saying 'we are at least given some ground for' I concede the weakness of my position. I have never supposed that I was arguing from a position of strength. My concern is with 'words, contexture, and other circumstances of Language', with language, judgement, and circumstance; not only the ways in which judgement is conveyed through language but also the difficulty of clearing the terms of judgement amid the mass of circumstance, the pressures of contingency. 'Cum autem intellectus acutior aut observatio diligentior res melius distinguere velit, verba obstrepunt' ['and where a more acute intellect or a more diligent observation tries to introduce a better distinction, words rebel']. But 'obstrepere' is literally 'to make a noise against', 'to shout down'. Against Bacon's exemplum of the Tartar's bow one may set the metaphor of the writer as a player upon an instrument: 'You have got to know exactly where you are going, aurally and physically[,] and then you have got to make exactly the right movement to take you there at the right time.'

> Two Paradises 'twere in one
> To live in Paradise alone.

This begins as paronomasia, according to Peacham's definition: 'Two/to', 'Paradises/Paradise', 'in one/alone'. But the energy of Marvell's figure is in direct opposition to the notion of 'declining into a contrary'; it is more an ascension into the positive. The particular beauty of these lines is their reconciling of the ephemeral, the elusive, with the 'knowing'. The strained metaphysical fancy which supposes that an inclusive exclusiveness is at one with an exclusive inclusiveness is made to sound so simply right, with such a singing felicity, that 'a more diligent observation' and 'a better distinction' appear to have been made, and made against the odds. The words do 'twist back' upon the understanding from which they proceeded but the imagination has already actively reconciled itself to this.

In referring to the 'strained metaphysical fancy' I intend both 'pushed beyond what is natural and reasonable' and 'purified' from grosser elements. The grossness is not merely the bulk, weight, density of contingent circumstance; it is also the palpable awkwardness of method: the negative, threatening paradox at the heart of 'Metaphysical' poetics is that the process of refining may itself be a gross piece of mechanics. 'Cribrate', meaning 'to sift', 'cribration', meaning 'sifting', are not words that have filtered through into common usage. Their meaning is that matters can be successfully refined and reduced but they obstruct their own claim. It is true that Donne more than once succeeds in turning the obstruction to advantage, as when he evokes the needful but awkward 'dissections, & cribrations, and examinings of Hereticall adventures upon' God's Word, or alerts his auditors to 'this examination, this agitation, this cribration, this pursuit of thy *conscience* to *sift* it, to follow it from the *sinnes* of thy *youth* to thy *present sinnes*', adding 'That's *time spent* like thy *Saviours.*' In a letter of April 1627 to Sir Robert Ker he discusses a sermon which has caused him much trouble. The trouble arose less from any theological perplexity (though the sermon has its grimly controversial moments) than from Donne's being drawn, against his own volition, into a quarrel between the Archbishop of Canterbury and William Laud, at that time Bishop of Bath and Wells; a quarrel in which the king strongly favoured Laud while Donne, on no good evidence, was suspected of supporting the Archbishop. Despite his acute intellect and diligent observation this sermon did cause offence and Donne wrote urgently to request Ker's mediation at Court, ruefully observing 'as Card. *Cusanus* wrote a book *Cribratio Alchorani*, I have cribrated, and re-cribrated, and post-cribrated the Sermon'. Donne's overemphasis of the already obtrusive term, clogging the process in the very effort to sift more finely, reads as a distressed parody of the perplexed circumstance, a travesty of his own anxious scholarship—its powerless exercise of powerful diligence and scruple, confronted by the 'prejudice' and 'displeasure' of the men of power.

If I say that all writers are bound to work with relative proportions of 'hefting' words to 'tuning' words I must immediately add that Hobbes's caveat 'all *metaphors* are by profession *equivocal*' still applies and that the same word may satisfy either attribute at one time or another: it is a matter of the drift and occasion and contexture of the speech. Words, generally, may be taken as hefting words 'such . . . as may serve for the upholding common Conversation and Commerce, about the ordinary Affairs and Conveniencies of civil Life', the approximate meanings, the jargon, that 'Men make a shift with, in the ordinary Occurrences of Life, where they find it necessary to be understood, and therefore they make signs till they are so'. John Locke's way of putting it, particularly apposite to this matter, is itself more than a mere shifting; it is a judicious weighing of an effect. Men do weigh their words pragmatically, albeit with more 'unsteady and confused Notions' than Locke's, in the furtherance of their 'Conveniencies', and his phrases settle themselves comfortably enough into the medium which they effectively describe and assess. By 'tuning' I mean to suggest something more than the Lockian ability to put words in their place. It has more affinity, as I understand it, with George Herbert's 'being true to [the] businesse'. His exemplary priest 'hath exactly sifted the definitions of all vertues, and vices; especially canvasing those, whose natures are most stealing, and beginnings uncertaine'. Herbert's 'hath exactly sifted' is of a different temper from Donne's 'cribrated, and re-cribrated, and post-cribrated' and is equally distinct from Locke's civil empirical precision. The Parson's eye establishes 'just occasion', mortifies covetousness, gluttony. Donne, in his letter to Ker, expresses mortification of a different kind; it is not Herbert's 'divine vertue' but an unhappy circumstance. He deliberately tunes in to the harshness, makes comically wretched 'business' out of a bad business. In 'Hymne to God, my God, in my sicknesse', on the other hand, when he writes 'Since I am comming to that Holy roome, | Where, with thy Quire of Saints for evermore, | I shall be made thy Musique', he is retuning and reconciling the afflicted man's angry, humiliated cry, in Lamentations, for divine retribution and restitution: 'Behold, their sitting downe, and their rising vp; I *am* their musicke', words which he himself glosses, in his verse-paraphrase 'The Lamentations of Jeremy', 'I am their song, whether they rise or sit.' From 'their musicke', 'their song', to 'thy Musique'; the tone of one who laments his sojourn in the enemy's country transposed to the melody of one who journeys to the celestial city.

The 'tuning' faculty involves tuning out as well as tuning in. The extent to which any writer is, or is not, aware of 'overtones', 'harmonics', in the language, the degree to which it is possible, necessary, or desirable for a reader to 'hear' the harmonics, are matters of nice speculation. Should I, or should I not, for instance, in my own choice of 'hefting', try to tune out all recollection of Leontes' 'violent Hefts' in Act II, scene i, of *The Winter's Tale*? I would agree that a judicious weighing of one's words might find intolerable such a grotesque eruption. On the other hand, an image of violent psychic and physical nausea is not inappropriate to an account of the always exhausting, at times mortifying and ignominious, struggle with language: 'verba obstrepunt.' 'I have cribrated, and re-cribrated, and post-cribrated.' What is this if not a series of violent hefts?

In Donne's Verse Letters to Sir Henry Wotton, in Marvell's parliamentary correspondence, the reciprocating stressfulness of what Hobbes calls 'the custom and common use of speech', at once ours and not ours, is encountered as a sense of persistent attrition. In the Verse Letters the harassment of the enduring images of worth, the moral images and examples, by the perversity and absurdity of 'habitual vice', 'egregious gests' (73–4), is engineered into a rhetoric that succeeds in retorting upon the perversity. It would be unjust to ask as much of Marvell's hastily written letters. 'I returned the civillest words that I could coyne at the present & renderd him your humble thanks for his continuall patronage of you'. So Marvell wrote to the Mayor of Hull, in November 1668, of his meeting with one of the king's generals. 'Coyne' is two-sided though not two-faced. It means, I take it, 'I made a genuine representation of your wishes out of the words that I was expected to utter, that it was expedient to say.' Words are simultaneously true specie and specious. Marvell writes with candour rather than with cynicism of an occasion on which both parties had weighed the business that demands our civillest words. In the lyric dialogues and soliloquies, mostly assumed to date from no later than the early 1650s, Marvell's finesse shows in his tuning in to the possibility of tuning out from this kind of 'business'. In those poems the word 'business' itself, to which he resorts so many times in his letters, does not feature except as the shadowy 'busie Companies of Men', somewhere out there, beyond the happy confines of 'The Garden'. The quick-wittedness needed to coin the civillest words one can contrive is still not the wit of 'Two Paradises 'twere in one | To live in Paradise alone.' There are two sentences in particular, from the letters of this period, which epitomize the attrition of circumstance upon judgement. In October 1666 he writes to the Mayor of Hull 'really busynesse dos so multiply of late that I can scarce snatch time to write to you'. Barely adumbrated in this hasty phrase is that Horatian theme which Marvell, a poet acutely aware of the perils and ecstasies of 'snatching time', had found so appealing.

35

But now there is no time, no *otium* amid the grinding
parliamentary *negotium*, for anything other than expedient
coining, no place for that gratuitous word-play which is at the
same time a considered judgement upon the world of business.
We do hear a brief wry reprise of that sense of 'precious Time'
some years later, in the letter 'To A Friend in Persia' of August
1671: 'Now, after my usual Method, leaving to others what
relates to Busyness, I address myself, which is all I am good for,
to be your Gazettier.' The friend was with the East India
Company and the letter is replete with business, though the
news is rattled through *alla burlesca* ('the *Bishop of Cullen* is
attacking the City of *Colen*' etc.).

In seventeenth-century English the word 'business' itself is
both hefted and tuned. It may have the function of shorthand:
'*Civill* or *Ecclesiasticall* businesse', 'office-business', 'publicke
businesse', 'law businesse', 'the businesse of the House'. It may
be a form of code. 'The Ballast businesse' and 'the French
Merchants businesse' briefly summarize lengthy parliamentary
investigations into malpractices. This usage shades imperceptibly,
through the matching of circumstance by circumspection, into
euphemism. There are matters best conveyed, as Sir Henry
Wotton observes, in the Venetian manner, '*sotto parole tacite*',
and 'business' is at times as good as a nod or a wink. 'My L:
Mordants businesse' alludes to an impeachment; 'the businesse
of Chatham' is parliament's enquiry into the national humiliation
suffered when the Dutch burnt the English fleet at anchor. There
is a further form of euphemism implicated in terror and cruelty.
'You are not ignorant of our Business with you' in Dryden's
Amboyna means 'I will not speak of the tortures to which we are
about to subject you, for they are, as you are aware, unspeakable.'
This is perhaps a particular 'aesthetic' application. In the affairs
and business of the world the word usefully compounds the
direct and oblique. When Pepys writes 'my Tanger=Boates
business' it is both a money-making venture and a euphemism
for the knowledge of his own bribe-taking, for the uneasy
negotiation between conscience and opportunism, greed and
fear. 'Business' can mean one's specific function, *métier*, a
commitment and obligation born of a particular aptitude—'For

the *Moral* (as *Bossu* observes) is the first business of the *Poet.*' This can flick into mockery when a Restoration theatre audience is informed ''tis your business to be couz'ned here'. The word's spectrum has, at one extreme, Clarendon's valediction to Falkland, at the other, Cromwell's words on hearing of the death of the Royalist Charles Cavendish '*We have donne our businesse.*' Clarendon writes of Falkland 'Thus fell, that incomparable younge man . . . havinge so much dispatched the businesse of life, that the oldest rarely attayne to that immense knowledge, and the youngest enter not into the world with more innocence'. 'Businesse' here comprehends the wise management of a great patrimony, the exemplary conduct of public affairs, the acquisition of a moral education through classical reading, and the practice of the established religion. It excludes the possibility that 'business' itself may be a word of curt dispatch, whereas Cromwell's '*businesse*' takes pleasure in the fact that it is so. Clarendon succeeds very well in what he is after: a conflation of the Virgilian '*mortalia*' ('For, this life, is . . . a businesse, and a perplext businesse', as Donne said) with Pauline exhortation ('Make you perfect in euery good worke to doe his will').

It may be objected that much of what I have to say ingenuously presumes that poets' apprehensions are what weigh and govern common daily experience and practice. My answer must be that 'Domestique affaires', in the 'sixteenth and seventeenth centuries, could comprehend such public matters as the day-to-day survival of the common weal, a 'Princely wakefulnesse', as Greville called it, in face of 'the dangerous temptations of power, wealth, and practice'. A further objection would make the point that, whether in Greville's *The Life of the Renowned Sr Philip Sidney* or in Dryden's letters, 'poetry' and 'Poetical' may be used to mean not 'reall', not genuine. Dryden assures the Earl of Chesterfield that the translation of the *Georgics* was dedicated to him 'from the bottom of my heart, and without poetry' (Ls 91). Such caveats were axiomatic. It was equally axiomatic, however, that the axioms themselves, the 'safe precepts of divine, and moral duty', were not, in fact, safe at all but were continually threatened by those agencies which the diplomatic Wotton epitomized as 'buisinesses and other accidents'. That 'all *metaphors* are by profession *equivocal*' can be taken as strengthening the opinion of those who understand 'Poetical' to mean fictitious or as supporting the view that the equivocal is, in any case, that which constitutes the reality of poetry's grasp upon protean matter.

Dryden remarks, in the first sentence of the 'Preface' to *All for Love*, that 'the death of *Anthony* and *Cleopatra*, is a Subject which has been treated by the greatest Wits of our Nation, after *Shakespeare*; and by all so variously, that their example has given me the confidence to try my self in this Bowe of *Ulysses* amongst the Crowd of Sutors; and, withal, to take my own measures, in aiming at the Mark' (13: 10). Dryden is equivocal. If Shakespeare is the one true master of the 'Bowe' then Dryden is one of the 'insolent' suitors, the 'devourers' of the Shakespearian patrimony. But, in Homer, none of the suitors can string the bow; the possession of that requisite strength is what sets Ulysses apart. Homer describes him trying the bow as another might tune a lyre. Dryden presents himself as if with the strung bow in his grasp, stepping forward, 'aiming at the Mark', taking his own 'measures'. With this phrase he comprehends the necessary expertise (like the 'aptnesse' and 'cunnynge' that Ascham's Toxophilus dilates upon) and the need to weigh and gauge his own abilities with a view to what he may expect of himself (as in the French 'prendre des mesures'). One is true to one's aim by taking one's true aim in the measures of a craft that is at once intimately one's own and not one's own. It is gratifying to observe that *All for Love* was written *con amore*. He would say of it 'I never writ any thing for my self but *Anthony and Cleopatra*'. In *The Elements of Architecture* Wotton remarks that '*Con Amore*' is one of 'three notable *Phrases*' in use 'among *Italian* Artizans'; he says that it means that something is done with 'a *loving diligence*' as distinct from 'a bare and *ordinary diligence*' or even 'a *learned diligence*'. 'They mean not with love to the *Bespeaker* of the *Worke*, but with a love and delight in the *Worke* it selfe'. Dryden and his fellow professionals wrote, for the most part, as 'Artizans' and most of the time, of necessity, with an eye 'to the *Bespeaker* of the *Worke*'. The wonder is that, with Dryden, again and again, the three modes of diligence 'concurre' as Wotton suggests that, 'in an eminent *Authour*', they should. In the 'Preface' to *All for Love* Dryden so handles the prescribed formalities that, within the space of a sentence, he moves from being an upstart competitor to one who feels that he has come home. The equivocation, therefore, does not preclude a proud certainty. It is a cursory formal nod in the direction of 'compleasance', the obligatory accommodation of critical opinion and of the rabble of one's so-called peers. It is also the necessary sense of occasion, the measuring of the moment when genius will step forward and declare itself. It is, too, the recognition that 'business' is not only the arbitrariness and attrition of the 'usuall traffique' but is also the firm grasp of common things. When the tuning and the hefting 'concurre' we know it, it is self-evident. To this extent we may say that Emerson is vindicated in his grand claim: 'Instantly we know whose words are loaded with life, and whose not.'

THREE

Caveats Enough in their Own Walks

AN apophthegm of Cicero claims that it is an error of judgement for statesmen to think and act as if they were living 'in Platonis πολιτείᾳ' and not 'in Romuli faece'. Bacon, in *The Advancement of Learning*, and Clarendon in his portrayal of Lord Falkland find it apposite to their didactic purposes, as does Pound in his sixty-fifth Canto. Bacon concedes that it may be a fault of 'learned men' to 'contend sometimes too farre, to bring thinges to perfection; and to reduce the corruption of manners, to honestie of precepts, or examples of too great height'. Yet, as he says, 'they haue Caueats ynough in their owne walkes'. Clarendon records that Falkland's friends 'did believe that he was of a temper and composition fitter to lyve in Republica Platonis then in faece Romuli; but this rigidnesse was only exercised towards himselfe, towards his frends infirmityes no man was more indulgent'. Between the self-imposed sanctions of a vulnerable 'rigidnesse' and the magnanimous tolerance for what Clarendon terms 'the common practice of men' the ethical terrain is ill defined but negotiable. One may distinguish broadly between those authors who, while concurring with Bacon's 'Caueats ynough in their owne walkes', none the less treat the caveat itself as one of many pertinent commonplaces and those whose concurrence is embodied in the contexture of the style itself.

Between 1597/8 and 1604 Donne addressed four 'Verse Letters' to his lifelong friend Henry Wotton. The last of these, 'To Sir Henry Wotton, at his going Ambassador to Venice' (75–6), is a poem of ten quatrains making what appears to be

41

an easy progress through the familiar formalities, formal familiarities, of Jacobean compliment. It claims and celebrates courteous acquaintance and advances the orthodox proposition that the king himself 'derives' (i.e. imparts, transmits) his 'soule', his 'vertue', to the obedient and grateful subject through the rites, the instruments, of hieratic fealty: in Wotton's case, the letters patent of his brand-new knighthood, and of his recent appointment, the credential letters which he duly presented to the Doge in September 1604. The poem acts as the diligent secretary to its own moral images and examples, referring in order of status, as though at some cabinet of privileged responsibility, to the 'reverend papers' bearing 'Our good and great Kings lov'd hand and fear'd name', the 'learned papers' of the scholar-diplomat himself, the 'loving papers', the farewell letters of friends and well-wishers, and finally the 'honest paper' of Donne's own valedictory, which both serves and subsumes the rest.

The conduct of the public estate, since it invests and has invested in it so much of one's own private state or condition, is, as Donne implies in his poems to Wotton, a 'knottie riddle' (71). Wotton was soon to discover the fitness of similar expressions. His dispatches from Venice, even while they furthered with exemplary devotion the interests of his 'Most Dear and Dread Soveraign' James I (A 384), were threaded with caveat and deploration concerning the politic entanglements of his 'ambassage'. He wrote frequently of 'this intricat buisinesse', 'the bowels of this perplexed buisinesse', 'the principall knott of the whole Businesse', 'one maine knott in the whole businesse'. Donne's 'knottie riddle' says compactly what several of his contemporaries had said, or were about to say, at greater length: it evokes the real labour of 'nosce teipsum'. Such a knot is a perplexing of several strands: lines of axiomatic prescription and proscription, sinews of present policy; there is, as Wotton advised, a proper 'tyme to knitt knotts'. Greville's *Life of the Renowned Sr Philip Sidney* upholds the ideal which, he argues, Sidney upheld: the attainment of a difficult 'ballance' between 'ambition' and the 'safe precepts of divine, and moral duty'. Wotton, in 1622, writes of the Prince of Condé and Paolo Sarpi in conference, of the Prince's pressing questions on certain difficult and delicate matters, and or Sarpi's answers 'holding a meane betweene confession and denyall, and yet w[it]hout equiuocation'. It is evident that Sarpi's dexterity in holding a mean between confession and denial is to be distinguished from Sidney's 'ballance' between ambition and precept though it is equally evident that they are comparable instances of '*Policie*', Bacon's 'most immersed' of knowledges. The apparently clear distinction between Wotton's desire 'to reduce . . . irregularities . . . to constant principles' (C 413) and Bacon's expressed dislike of 'that which taketh the way, to reduce Learning to certaine emptie and barren Generalities' is deceptive. There are reserves of irony in Wotton's manner when he contemplates the ethics of the Jacobean Court. Bacon, who reservedly admired Machiavelli's up-to-date grasp of the 'cose del mondo', resembled the Italian theorist in his command of the ancient maxims and exempla. He seems no less 'beholden' to Cicero than he is to '*Macciauell &* others that write what men doe and not what they ought to do'. If 'doe' is the 'common practice of men' then 'ought' is the 'rigidnesse' which was to bring the gentle Falkland to such distress.

Once the idea of 'rigidnesse' has been accommodated it may become malleable. One may have an ironic stoicism of style in which a 'seueare' love of justice and a 'praecise' love of truth, the 'examples of too great height', seem conscious of their marginal status. In May 1613 Wotton wrote from London to Sir Edmund Bacon in the country with news of an action before the Star Chamber. He remarked that the Lord Privy Seal, believing himself defamed in a private letter, 'hath been moved besides his own nature, and (as some think also) besides his wisdom, to call these things into publick discourse; *quae spreta exolescunt*, if ancient grave Sentences do not deceive us' (C 411). The gist of this, both in the Latin and in Wotton's gloss, is that if you disdain contumely it will be quickly forgotten; if you react angrily it will stick. The ancient grave sentences heard wryly exclaiming from the wings of this worldly theatre appear to be those of Tacitus' *Annals*, iv. 34: a rehearsing of some words from the apologia of the doomed historian Cremutius Cordus, impeached by Sejanus' minions and condemned by Tiberius. This rhetorical set piece argues that despotic attempts to destroy truth-telling books succeed only in heaping the tyrants with ignominy and their victims with renown. Seneca wrote *Ad Marciam: De Consolatione* for the daughter of Cordus, a piece in which the rigidness of her father's virtue is grasped by a brief implacable phrase: '. . . proscribentes in aeternum ipse proscripsit.' There is no room for negotiation in that grammatical lock. Yet in Wotton's 'if ancient grave Sentences do not deceive us' such austere rectitude, to which undoubtedly he gave entire assent, receives the tincture of some quaint and harmless pedantry: 'I take pleasure (speaking to a Philosopher) to reduce (as near as I can) the irregularities of Court to constant principles' (C 413). This suggestion that attention to 'constant principles' is to be equated with private 'pleasure', even with amateurishness ('as near as I can'), may appear a gesture of wry helplessness. It is rather a steely diffidence, which will not accede to indifference, which accepts the fact that judgement may be disadvantaged by circumstance, and which trusts to style to have the last word— literally, one may say, for in his last will and testament Wotton requested, in a series of sharply civil phrases, 'the solicitation of my Arrears' (A c11), indicating that his outstanding debts should be paid by his executors out of the salary that was still owing to him. His biographer Izaac Walton catches the nuance in his comment that 'a doubt still remains, whether it discovered more *holy wit*, or *conscionable policy*' (A c7ᵛ), though it is to be noted that in the following sentence he feels obliged to reduce that equivocation to an unambiguously pious sentiment. Virtually in the same breath he vindicates Wotton's judgement and compromises with the circumstance.

Bacon wrote that 'the wit and minde of man, if it worke vpon matter, which is the contemplation of the creatures of God worketh according to the stuffe, and is limited thereby'. Walton's own art, in *The Compleat Angler*, constitutes a *via media* between the 'wit' of man and the 'matter', between axiom and experiment, between virtue-in-contemplation and virtue-in-action. It is Bacon's 'diligent and exquisite . . . Historie of liuing creatures' made manifest in the spinning of a pleasant yarn. But experiment here substantiates Ecclesiastes' axiom that '*Every thing is beautifull in his season.*' Bacon, in *The Advancement of Learning*, had quoted the words with equal pleasure. At their finest, as well as at their most fidgety, the Anglican Royalists manipulate a responsive thread between the wit and mind of their sentiments and that matter, of which language is a part, contemplated in its most minute particulars. Clarendon precisely qualifies the 'flowinge delightfulnesse' of Falkland's language with the 'chast[ness]' of his 'tounge and eare'. Walton prefers 'doing that natural office' (295) for acts of copulation between the creatures which Aubrey cheerily calls 'bussinesse'. For Walton the communion of nature with man is itself like that 'convivium philosophicum' or 'convivium theologicum' to which Clarendon compared the conversation of Falkland.

Aldrovandus says . . . all fish that live in clear and sharp streames, are made by nature their mother of such exact shape and pleasant colours, purposely to invite us to a joy and contentednesse in feasting with her . . . *Salvian* [takes the Umber to be so called] from his swift swimming or gliding out of sight, more like a shadow or a Ghoste then a fish. Much more might be said both of the smell and taste, but I shal only tell you, that Saint *Ambrose* the glorious Bishop of *Millan* (who liv'd when the Church kept Fasting dayes) calls him the *flowre fish*, or flowre of fishes . . .

Walton's finesse is shown here in his keeping a due respect between the connotations of 'sharp' and 'pleasant'. A natural 'joy and contentednesse' is sanctified by the pronouncing of Saint Ambrose's name; our appetite for the 'feast' is both chastened and whetted by the salutary proximity of the 'fast'. An admirer of Herbert's 'Sweet day, so cool, so calm, so bright', Walton writes as if he takes it for a paradigm. That poem's generous and obsequious compliance is anticipated by Piscator's words to his scholar Viator ('nay and the earth smels as sweetly too') and, the song–recital completed, Viator speaks in the aural afterglow of Herbert's words ('I thank you, good Master . . . for the sweet enjoyment of the pleasant day' 111–12).

When this book first appeared, however, it was far from being a pleasant day for Royalist Anglicans. That condition of felicity to which both Walton and Clarendon appeal is retrospective and pre-emptive. Clarendon is a special pleader and Walton's angling is at times the *via media* between ingenuousness and the disingenuous. That which Walton successfully retrieves in passages of *The Compleat Angler* and the *Lives* . . . is the Jacobean and Caroline Anglican comeliness. That spirit, itself at odds with the frequent dereliction of ecclesiastical duties and fabrics, is epitomized by George Wither's 'Song XIII' ('Oh my *Loue*, how comely now') of *The Hymnes and Songs of the Church*, 'plainely and briefly express[ing] in *Lyricke-verse*' the exuberant equivocal metaphors of The Song of Solomon, which Orlando Gibbons provided with 'Musicke agreeable to the matter'. 'Comeliness' is a quality pre-eminently celebrated in Donne's tribute to the memory of Magdalen Herbert, Lady Danvers, George Herbert's mother: 'To this consideration of her *person* then, belongs this, that *God* gave her such a *comelinesse*, as, though shee were not *proud* of it, yet she was so content with it, as not to goe about to mend it, by any *Art* . . . Her *rule* was *mediocrity*'. Its pervasiveness is traceable in Wotton's favouring 'apt *Coherence*, without *distraction*, without *confusion*', an architecture that keeps 'a due *Respect* between the *Inhabitant* and the *Habitation*' (A 259, 304), in Clarendon's praise of Falkland's 'generous and obsequious complyance with all good men', together with Walton's love of 'choice Song, and sweetly sung' (90), of the 'good, plain, unperplext Catechism, that is printed with the old Service Book' (76), and of what he calls 'the most honest, ingenious, harmless Art of Angling' (69). The tactical paradox self-evidently turns on the notion of 'art', on the attainment of a skilled artlessness which, while not 'contemptible to men of best vnderstandings', is ideally 'what the Common apprehension can best admit'. Wither is at pains to stress not only that he and Gibbons have eschewed 'the curious Fancies of the Time' but also that to have kept to the 'curious' mode would have been the easier way. Walton's own 'ingenious' art, like the word itself in seventeenth-century English, is not always what it may seem.

The Life of Sir Henry Wotton appeared in 1651 as the preface to the first edition of *Reliquiae Wottonianae*. *The Compleat Angler* was published two years later. The exemplary figure to whom tribute is offered in both books is the man who has fought his way through defeats and pyrrhic victories to achieve, at last, a felicitous mediocrity between contemplation and action, conscience and policy; a felicity for which the art of angling provides at once the mystical ideal and the practical exercise. It is as if Walton, in tuning and tempering his own style, has chosen to identify with the persona of Wotton's late, retired meditations. In 1651 he depicts Wotton daily praising God for a 'particular *Mercy*' (A c5ᵛ); in 1654 the record is more precise and more expansive; it is the 'particular mercy, of an exemption from busines' (B 60). *The Compleat Angler* is wholly in sympathy with this mood of 'exemption'. It pleases Walton to appear as a stubbornly conservative poetry-lover. 'Old fashioned Poetry, but choicely good' he observes of songs by the once brilliantly threatening libertine 'atheists' Marlowe and Ralegh (89). Donne, the subject of one of Walton's *Lives*, appears in *The Compleat Angler* merely as the author of that pert parody 'The Baite', cited to show that 'hee could make soft and smooth Verses, when he thought them fit and worth his labour' (137–8). In the first and second editions Walton claims that Marlowe's and Ralegh's verse was 'much better then that now in fashion in this Critical age' (89). In the third edition of 1661 this becomes 'much better then the strong lines that are now in fashion in this criticall age'. But 'strong lines', a Jacobean 'metaphysical' predilection persisting in the 'strong Expressions' of Cleveland and his imitators, were even less in favour in 1661 than they had been in 1653 or 1655. Old-fashioned Walton is not so stubborn as to be out of step with shifting prejudice, a new strength of opinion which dismisses 'strong lines' as 'no better then Riddles' and deplores all ventures into 'palpable darknesse' and 'ambitious obscurity'.

There are, none the less, intimations in *The Compleat Angler* that Walton is not unaware that his 'ingenious Art' lets down a thread from the bright day into a 'palpable darkness' 'where the water is deep, and runs quietly' (146). Wotton certainly thought of diplomacy as angling. 'At this the Fish did not bite' he noted, of some rejected political feeler. Among the authors of 'Commendatory Verses' added to the second edition of Walton's book were those who pondered the reciprocal connection: 'Vagos honesta fraude pisces decipis' (432). To practise on 'these creatures' the arts of ensnarement is an innocent form of policy: 'Fish from your arts do rescue men' (429). When you have spliced the live frog on your line, Piscator advises, as though floating one of Machiavelli's maxims, 'use him as though you loved him . . . that he may live the longer' (126). It is as if Walton's awareness of the duplicitous world is itself divided, partly into the practical management of his line, partly into the security of well-tried commonplace: 'you will find angling to be like the vertue of Humility, which has a calmness of spirit, and a world of other blessings attending upon it' (205–6). It is reminiscent of Greville's 'reciprocall Paradise of mutuall humane duties' or Wotton's, or Donne's, tributes to 'mediocrity' and 'due Respect'. There is, however, another kind of middle way which Walton is less inclined to admit into the contemplation of English poetry or the advocacy of English virtue: the 'betwixt' of constraint, enforcement, or perplexity, heard in Lear's 'To come betwixt our sentence and our power', or the 'Epitaph on the Earl of Strafford' ('Huddled up 'twixt Fit and Just . . . 'Twixt Treason and Convenience'), in Marvell's 'But Fate does Iron wedges drive, | And alwaies crouds it self betwixt', and in Eugenius' opinion that Ovid excelled in showing 'the various movements of a Soul combating betwixt two different Passions'. This is a region into which Walton dips, from time to time, with equivocal metaphors but refrains from taking up into the domain of 'reason . . . worthy the consideration of a wise man' (82).

In a letter from Venice to a friend in England Wotton wrote 'In the mean while till his Majestie shall resolve me again into mine own plaine and simple elements, I have abroad done my poor endeavour according to these occasions which God hath opened' (A 406). The way of life of the later Wotton is that of one who has happily returned upon his own prescience, who has had the resolution to be resolved into 'plaine and simple elements', finding his happiness in the dissolution of worldly promises and hopes. It is this spirit that Walton, in *The Life of Sir Henry Wotton* and *The Compleat Angler*, offers to his readers as the essence of the moral life. In Wotton's testament, as in his recorded *bons mots*, eloquence and readiness of conceit, previously whetted on dangerous circumstance, have been largely exempted from such business, either by Walton's tact in associating 'holy' and 'conscionable' with 'wit' and 'policy' or by their own withdrawal into a self-sustaining reflective mannerism: 'Nor did he forget his innate pleasure of *Angling*; which he would usually call, his idle time not idly spent' (A c6).

Walton enhances the felicities of exempted wit by demonstrating what it has been exempted from: for instance, that 'accident' at the outset of Wotton's diplomatic career when his wit placed him in jeopardy and 'much clouded' his prospects of royal favour; that 'pleasant definition' '*Legatus est vir bonus peregrè missus ad mentiendum Reipublicae causa*' which he 'could have been content should have been thus Englished. *An Embassadour is an honest man sent to lie abroad for the good of his Countrey*'. However, 'the word for *lie* (being the hinge upon which the Conceit was to turn) was not so express'd in Latin as would admit (in the hands of an enemy especially) so fair a Construction as Sir *Henry* thought in *English*' (A c1ᵛ). Wotton's and Walton's discovery of an inoperative 'hinge' anticipates Pound's remark that '*logopoeia*' is a 'tricky and undependable mode' which 'does not translate' and it is not out of sympathy with Bacon's caveat about 'delicacies and affectations', vanity of style, the ambition to make things seem more ingenious than they really are. In *The Life of Wotton*, as in *The Compleat Angler*, Walton is reluctant to appear over-ingenious or to 'break the rules of Civility' (183) or of 'discretion' (63). Familiar as he is with the conventional workings of the line of wit ('I have made a recreation, of a recreation' 59), there are a number of semantic hazards and opportunities with which he does not engage, a particular box of tricks which he itemizes but does not take up. Although, in 1661, he dismisses the 'strong lines' of the suspect Metaphysicals, he continues to urge the value of strong lines to his own ingenious-ingenuous Art: 'And you must Fish for him with a strong Line', 'take a strong small hook tied to a strong line' (318). He is either not aware of, or not interested in, the ironic possibilities of the collocation. Herbert's 'box where sweets compacted lie' means much to him but the suggestiveness

49

of another box is left where he found it, with Wotton's holy wit
or conscionable policy: that '*Chest, or* Cabinet *of Instruments and
Engines of all kinds of uses*' bequeathed by Wotton to a close
friend, 'in the lower box whereof, are some fit to be bequeathed
to none but so entire an honest man as he is'. According to
Walton's marginal note: 'In it were *Italian* locks, pick-locks,
screws to force open doors; and things of worth and rarity, that
he had gathered in his forrain Travell' (A c10ᵛ). Even 'holy
Mr *Herbert*' (111), who was not shy of matching the strings of
his lute to the 'stretched sinews' of his crucified Lord, would
have sensed something ponderable there. For Walton, 'the very
sinews of vertue' are not strong lines or the lute's 'struggle' for
its 'part' with all its 'art'; they are, as he says, 'good company
and good discourse' (214). That safe platitude marks the extent
of the 'exemption' which he permits himself and those on whose
behalf he writes.

In Donne's four verse letters to Wotton one finds, even more
than 'crabbed and ambiguous syntax' and the stretched sinews of
conceit, a recognition of the simple rightness of things of virtue,
which none the less has to be grasped through 'incongruity' (74),
by way of the 'crooked' (74), the 'adverse' (71), the 'extremes'
(71). In the third letter, 'H.W. in Hiber[nia] Belligeranti' (74–5),
Donne engineers a conceit out of the curve-necked alchemical
vessels, the 'crooked lymbecks', to argue that the morally
crooked world may be made to retort upon itself, may be the
means of the soul's self-purification. In the second letter he
names the 'seely honesty' and 'neat integritie' of those who, 'in
this worlds warfare', are doomed as 'Indians 'gainst Spanish
hosts' (73). The epithets both mock and commiserate with the
ill-fated petitioners, comprehending their ingenuousness and the
world's ingenuities. Donne perceives that the medium of
language must itself be conceived as a 'crooked lymbeck'. To
claim that his particular poetic virtue leaves not a hair's-breadth
between moral principle and poetic practice is a half-truth unless
one adds that his practice is to find fit expression for the
unfittedness of 'Countries, Courts, Towns' (71) to lives of
rectitude. He writes, in the first of the set, that we are
unavoidably stained by the things 'wee must touch' (71); in the

last he adds 'Wee must for others vices care' (76). What is 'care'? To care is 'to take thought for' and 'to know sorrow for' and 'to be of service to'. Are we to serve the vices of others, or to suffer pain for them, or to be wounded by the knowledge of our servitude?

In 'To Sir Henry Wotton, at his going Ambassador to Venice' the celebration of a plain virtue seems a plain audacity:

> But though she [Fortune] part us, to heare my oft prayers
> For your increase, God is as neere me here;
> And to send you what I shall begge, his staires
> In length and ease are alike every where.

(76)

Such audacity is to be distinguished from the pleasant effrontery of Wotton's unlucky *jeu d'esprit*. 'God is as neere me here' strikes the note of that direct steadfastness which we are to believe the author found in his departing friend. Yet simple power has not been simply achieved. To reach this point Donne has had to take the measure of a politic jargon ('derives', 'command', 'admit', 'audience', 'your honour', 'businesse', 'Courts and Warres', 'Spies' (vb.), 'staires') as well as of his own wounded ambition. As Walton observed, years later, when he inserted this poem into the second (1654) edition of *Reliquiae Wottonianae*, 'his dear friend Dr *Donne*, (then a private Gentleman) was not one of that number that did personally accompany him in this voyage' (B 36). To compare and contrast Walton's brisk parenthetical tact with Donne's scarcely tactful parentheses—'For mee (if there be such a thing as I) | Fortune (if there be such a thing as shee)'—is to remark how the individual poetic voice can, and must, realize its own power amid, and indeed out of, that worldly business which makes certain desires and ambitions unrealizable. Donne addresses Wotton, about to embark on the further hazards of the world, as a man who has already creditably encountered a number of the world's hazards '(Schooles and Courts and Warres o'rpast)', ''Tis therefore well your spirits now are plac'd | In their last Furnace, in activity'. Compare and contrast Wotton's own 'it is now too late to put me in a new Furnace' (A 392). The 'furnace' of alchemical 'activity' which is also the 'furnace of aduersitie' in Ecclesiasticus (chapter 2, verse 5) where 'acceptable menne' show their worth like gold, will further purify qualities in Wotton that are already well tried and that, in turn, will prove the metal of those with whom he comes in contact. It is what Davenant will later call 'the painfull activenesse of Vertue'. To claim that what is to be purified is already sufficiently pure through the exercise of learned discipline ('From which rich treasury you may command | Fit matter whether you will write, or doe') is to risk labouring the matter to the point where labour becomes otiosity. In the 'activity' of the poem, however, we are convinced that the nature of the moral life is an integrated process and that such retrospection is no less active than is Wotton's imminent diplomatic itinerary:

> . . . To sweare much love, not to be chang'd before
>   Honour alone will to your fortune fit;
> Nor shall I then honour your fortune, more
>   Then I have done your honour wanting it.   (76)

Although Donne's poem presents his friend as a man whose integrity fully justifies the tribute, the strenuous play of such argument is something from which Wotton's own style gently unperplexes itself, as in the letter from Venice some six years later. 'In the mean while till his Majestie shall resolve me again into mine own plaine and simple elements' makes a diplomat's *congé* out of the old scholastic physics that Marlowe's Faustus, in his last agony, so frantically clawed at; and contrives to imply that the 'plain and simple' are fated to appear pedantic and outmoded in a world devoted to other matters. Such words reflect the style of guarded amateurism which astute professionals, wishing to appear harmless, find desirable to cultivate in certain circumstances. It is a form of self-containment under duress. While Wotton in his own practice of this ingeniously ingenuous art is superior to his later belletristic admirers who seem unable to take seriously the relation of judgement to circumstance, he is none the less, in his elaborate self-exemptions, his apparently 'plain and simple' gestures, particularly vulnerable to their naïve or insouciant patronage. The Rt. Hon. H. H. Asquith, in his presidential address to the English Association in 1919, offers himself as a 'somewhat threadbare amateur' yet pronounces magisterially on what he calls 'the sovereign quality of Style'. 'Style', which is 'incommunicable, almost indefinable, never mistakable', is epitomized for Mr Asquith by Wotton's 'incomparable lines "On his Mistress, the Queen of Bohemia" '. Logan Pearsall Smith, in 1907, observes of the same poem:

> [W]ritten by an ambassador in an idle moment at Court, to a princess in whose service he was about to start on an impossible mission, [this] . . . bit of verse . . . takes its place among the most lovely of English lyrics. . . . Neither Queen nor ambassador probably gave, amid the cares of state, a second thought to the little poem. Yet, such is the magic of art, these verses have done more than anything else, perhaps, to make both of them remembered.

'Such is the magic of art', 'among the most lovely of English lyrics', embody two contradictory ideals which the patron finds equally appealing and would be pleased to reconcile to his personal satisfaction. The first is that poetry is essentially non-negotiable, it issues from 'idle moments' parenthetically enjoyed 'amid the cares of state' and to them it returns. It speaks from and to the '*otium*' not the '*negotium*'. The second is that, when all the worldly damage has been done, when cynicism and opportunism have had free reign, the 'magic' will be rediscovered wonderfully undiminished, parenthetically preserved, as though in some trust-fund or privileged continuity, 'incommunicable, almost indefinable, never mistakable'. 'Such is the magic of art', 'among the most lovely of English lyrics', presume, through otiosity, to confer a mystical status and authority on an art which is, through the agency of such cant, retained on the margins of the 'ordinary Affairs and Conveniences of civil Life'.

It is necessary, and necessarily chastening, to have to return upon the undeniable fact that neither Wotton nor his biographer Walton show themselves over-concerned with questions of poetic authority or status. Wotton affects to regard poetry either as a servant of the 'wanton cries' of 'Youth' or as ineffectual 'Plaints' barely audible above the real cries of loss:

> But is He gon? and live I Ryming here,
> As if some Muse would listen to my Lay . . .
>
> (A 528)

He writes to Sir Edmund Bacon that 'Surprizal' by political 'businesses' 'hath disturbed my Muses so' (C 414) and even *The Elements of Architecture* is called 'these vacant Observations' (A 297). This show of diffidence was required of a gentleman; but in Wotton's case the mannerism has been chosen with some forethought. 'On his Mistris, the Queen of Bohemia', written in 1619 or 1620 and suggested by some phrases of Petrarch, catches a reflection from the world of Wotton's 'forraign imployments in the service of this Nation', in particular, from 'the *Bohemian* businesse', 'the *Bohemian* Motions' (A 367–8), which so marred the happiness and fortune of his beloved Elizabeth, daughter of James I and wife to the Elector Palatine. It does not, however, reflect back upon those 'imployments', that 'businesse', those 'Motions', but upon something else:

> You meaner *Beauties* of the *Night* . . .
> You *Common people* of the *Skies*;
> What are you when the *Moon* shall rise?

The rhetorical question is a defiant affirmation, in tune with his customary style of address to her: '*Most Resplendent Queen, even in the Darknesse of Fortune*' (A 494), '. . . *Of cleer and resplendent vertues through the clouds of her Fortune*' (A c10), 'and even by her obscurity the more resplendent' (A 156). The poem is therefore a cameo, a miniature, of an apotheosis: his exaltation of that 'Image of [her] excellent Vertues' which, as he confessed to her, he had long since taken 'into [his] heart' (A 494). This form of exaltation is itself an exemption. When Milton addresses Henry Lawes—'Thy worth and skill exempts thee from the throng'— that worth, that skill, are not an incommunicable '*Eclypse and Glory*'. Wotton's lyric adoration is held reserved from the matter that surrounds it, the harsh circumstances of 'the *Bohemian* businesse', as he clearly believed the subject of his address was to be held inviolably aloof from the sordid and bitter intrigues that had plunged her into the '*Darknesse of Fortune*'. In being so preferred above the '*Common people* of the *Skies*' the object of adoration is also raised above the common practice of men and above the routine idioms of Wotton's own diplomatic correspondence ('the businesse of *Bohemia*' (A 372)).

Shortly after completing this poem Wotton was engaged, as James's ambassador extraordinary to Vienna, in the hopeless task of attempting to reconcile the Elector Palatine to the Emperor Ferdinand. At the conclusion of the negotiations the Emperor presented him with a 'Jewell of Diamonds of more worth then a thousand pounds'. Though Wotton received it 'with all tearms of honour' (which in subsequent revisions became 'all Circumstances and terms of Honour' and then 'all outward Circumstances and Terms of Honour') he none the less gave it away the next morning, declaring 'an indisposition to be the better for any gift that came from an enemy to his Royall Mistress; for so the Queen of *Bohemia* was pleas'd he should call her'. In so turning an honour received into a rebuke delivered Wotton was perhaps guided by the diplomatic practice of the time, but he also drew upon those qualities which he praised exemplary statesmen for possessing and which he himself possessed in good measure: 'great dexteritie in the conduct of affayres a cleere and extemporal iudgment much eloquence, and reddinesse of conceyte'. In 'On His Mistris, the Queen of Bohemia' it is as if the poet has elected to forgo the 'great dexterity', the 'clear and extemporal judgement', the active 'eloquence and readiness of conceit' appropriate to the *negotium*, the 'Motions', while retaining 'all outward Circumstances and Terms of Honour' in the beautifully set but conventional imagery of exaltation. The trope from which it derives is typified by the 'rich Iewel in an Æthiops eare: | Beauty too rich for vse, for earth too deare' of *Romeo and Juliet*. Wotton's poem is the equivalent of the 'Jewell of Diamonds of more worth then a thousand pounds' if that jewel had been simply retained and displayed, if it had not been put to 'use', in an instance of 'clear and extemporal judgement', made the 'hinge' upon which an effective diplomatic 'conceit' was to 'turn'.

Wotton, who knew what it was to suffer the forgetfulness and withdrawal of those in high places, emulates the art of courtly, masque-like self-withdrawal in the self-referential rhetorical questions of the poem: 'Tell me, if *she* were not design'd | Th' *Eclypse* and *Glory* of her kind?', questions to which there is no effectual answer. Assent would be otiose, dissent *lèse-majesté*. It is a lyricism contrasting sharply with the unlyrical tone of the verse letters addressed to him by John Donne. In these the language is awkwardly self-alerting to the nature of moral and linguistic circumstance, where the 'state' of the individual touches 'points of conuenience, and accommodating for the present' which, says Bacon, 'the Italians call *Ragioni di stato*'; in Machiavelli's terms, 'l'órdine delle cose', 'le cose del mondo', 'i tempi e le cose'. It is from such 'affayres of the world' that Wotton's lyricism, both by personal choice and by proxy, is exempted. 'To exempt' is literally 'to take out' and, in *The Compleat Angler*, he is indeed taken out and set down 'quietly in a Summers evening on a bank a fishing' (76). Walton here repeats some of Wotton's verse 'because it glides as soft and sweetly from his pen, as that River does now by which it was then made' (ibid.). It is, as we have observed, a characteristic of Walton's own style to glide softly and sweetly away from the proximity of too curious confrontations: 'I might say more of this, but it might be thought curiosity or worse' (124). 'A peece of meritoriouse curiositie' is Wotton's bland allusion to his own work in intercepting and deciphering the correspondence of Jesuits and other disaffected Catholics. 'Honest industrie' is another smoothly unhappy term for the practice ('I call that honest which tendeth to the discouerie of such as are not so by what meanes soeuer while I am uppon the present occupation'). This sentence is enough to refute Logan Pearsall Smith's claim that Wotton's diplomatic correspondence reveals 'how whole-heartedly, in becoming a diplomatist, he had adopted the morality of that profession'. A 'wholehearted' man would not need to gloss 'honest' so wryly. He is reported as observing, in his last days, *'though I have been and am a man compass'd about with humane frailties, Almighty God hath by his grace prevented me from making shipwrack of faith and a good Conscience'* (C e4). Such sentiments run parallel to poetic commonplace as to 'the safe precepts of divine and moral duty'. But Wotton, who so equivocated with the word 'honest', would know that language is more than a discreet courier between *de facto* circumstance and *de jure* commitments. As much as a man himself, a man's language is 'enter'd into very intrinsecal Familiarity' with 'dangerous matter'.

Among Plutarch's *Moralia* there is an essay of which Henry Vaughan published a translation, in 1651, with the title *Of the Benefit Wee may get by our Enemies*. We benefit, according to Plutarch, from being reviled and traduced by those who hate us, for by such harsh means one comes to know oneself. 'Where our wellwishers will give us no Councell, wee must make use of our Enemies words, and by a discreet application advantage our selves.' Equally, we are to guard against that 'vitious unfolding of our selves, extenuated with an Apologie of *a word escaped from me*, or, *I slipt a word unawares*' which 'never happens but to lavish, irresolute persons who by reason of their infirmitie of judgment, or loose Custome of life, stick alwaies in the same errours'. Walton recounts Wotton's misfortune as if it were an addendum to Plutarch's essay, emphasizing the readiness with which 'the hands of an Enemy' will distort one's fair constructions. The witticism, we are told, 'slept quietly . . . almost *eight years*' until 'by accident' it fell into the hands of a 'Romanist', a controversialist who used it in polemic against King James and the English Church (A c2). The *Life* further records that Wotton eventually righted himself with his royal master by an apology 'so ingenuous, so cleer, so choicely eloquent' that the king declared him to have 'commuted sufficiently for a greater offence' (A c2). Such whimsical largess is one of the innumerable perquisites of real power. Wotton writes as one who knows, by experience, the savage indifference that cohabits with an occasional magnanimity and who is attuned, by faith and learning, to the 'ancient grave sentences' that do not deceive us. In *The Elements of Architecture*, acknowledging Pliny the Elder's discourse on Greek and Roman statuary, he writes 'And true it is indeed, that the *Marble Monuments & Memories* of wel deserving Men, wherewith the very high ways were *strewed* on each side, was not a bare and transitory Entertainment of the *Eye*, or only a gentle deception of *Time* to the *Traveller*: But had also a secret and strong *Influence*, even into the advancement of the *Monarchy*, by continuall representation of vertuous Examples; so as in that

point, ART became a piece of *State*' (A 292–3). The tone here is
smoother than the circumstances which it accommodates.
'Continual' implies unbroken succession, a civic consensus
stretching from republican times well into the period of the
Caesars ('even into the advancement of the *Monarchy*'). But
Wotton, who had alluded to that passage in Tacitus' *Annals*
where Cremutius Cordus accuses his accusers, would know that
in the same speech Cordus pointedly refers to the venerated
statues of the dead Brutus and Cassius 'quas ne victor quidem
abolevit'. Various passages in Tacitus and others suggest that
Augustus, and later Trajan, showed a politic limited tolerance of
such veneration, which was, for the most part, exercised in
discreet privacy. The careful Latin distinctions between public
proscription and private exemption are elided, in Wotton's
historical synopsis, to a 'secret' influence exerted in public
places. Those Romans who retained republican sentiments 'even
into the advancement of the *Monarchy*' kept a sense of 'vertue'
different from that currently in vogue, and dismissed Augustan
modes of conduct as 'adulatio' and 'avaritia'. What, then, is
Wotton's 'continuall representation of vertuous Examples'? And
how does he envisage art as 'a piece of State'? In its most
apparent sense it is to be seen as an ancillary of civic didacticism,
a piece of the consensus; but when Cremutius Cordus, facing his
unjust judges, honours the memory of Brutus and Cassius by
speaking of their revered effigies his speech, like those statues, is
a piece of state in a different sense. It is a piece of unassimilated
matter lodged in the body politic and Wotton, in 1613, lodges a
fragment of it in his own observation on current *flagitia*. His
particular quality is to have annexed, for 'vertuous examples', a
style which the *Annals* associate with the enigmatic pronounce-
ments of a tyrant. Like Tiberius he uses 'verba . . . pauca et sensu
permodesto', though to the end of undercutting and outwitting
'Tiberius'. It is in more than one sense, however, a modest
achievement and Hobbes's recommendation that we should take
'the *drift*, and *occasion*, and *contexture*' (H 51) of a speech seems
particularly apposite. Wotton turns 'drift' into a form of stylistic
exemption and there is a limit to what can be done with 'gentle
deception'. Ben Jonson, who, in Act III of *Sejanus*, closely

paraphrases Cordus' speech from the *Annals*, is full and direct where Wotton is laconic and oblique. On the other hand, drama, with its formal dénouement, is a medium especially well suited to dealing with the just and unjust types of humanity represented in the writings of Tacitus and Plutarch, that 'vitious unfolding of our selves' which Jacobean and Restoration dramatists excelled in depicting. A word 'slipt . . . unawares' in a letter, a dispatch, or a treatise, or in the course of an evening's entertainment among those in whose hands one could not trust one's life, is a different matter from the theatrical presentation of 'lavish, irresolute persons' or 'words with words reueng'd'.

Literary handbooks encourage the assumption that Donne's poetry was not considered 'metaphysical' until Dryden, in 1692, used the phrase 'affects the Metaphysicks' (604) to conjure up an old-fashioned, quaintly intricate mode of writing. This assumption ignores the fact that, in the *Essayes in Divinity*, Donne had coined the term 'meta-theology' to denote 'a profounder theology than that recognized by divines'. The analogy here is palpable; self-evidently affecting the metaphysics, conscious that it is 'mis-interpretable; since to some palates it may taste of Ostentation'. The knotty riddling of Donne's verse and prose moves from, and through, rhetorical bravado and 'alarums' (he himself enters that caveat) to an engagement with meta-poetics, a profounder poetry than that recognized by conventional instructors in rhetoric and conduct. There is a letter of *c.*1600, attributed to him, which is taken as referring to his early 'Paradoxes': 'they are but swaggerers: quiet enough if you resist them.' It is no simple matter to describe and celebrate honour, constancy, or even a mere life-and-death seriousness of mind, in figures notoriously associated with the impertinent, the irreverent, the parodic ('When thou hast done, thou hast not done'). There is none the less an irreducible paradox or oxymoron in the mundane constitution, and the literary paradox is a formal submission that 'things' are so: 'they have beene written in an age when any thing is strong enough to overthrow [truth].' Such a discovery had itself been anticipated by Wyatt ('But what thynge is that that these mene wolde not wreste for there purpose that wreste suche thynges') and by Nashe ('There is nothing that if a man list he may not wrest or peruert'). Wyatt's 'what thynge', Nashe's 'nothing', Donne's 'any thing', are phrases of the most menial hefting recognized for what they are: tokens and agents of protean callousness. Tyrannical cunning and tyrannized intelligence are accommodated equally, though without equity, in such terms. 'Meta-poetry', as I labour to define it, challenges Bacon's 'Policie' as the most 'immersed' of crafts or 'knowledges' while resisting the cynical fatalism that may accompany the 'logical' liberation of the mind. Meta-poetry is immersed in the knowledge that it is so immersed. To be thus immersed in knowledge is not the same as to be steeped in axiomatic wisdom and experience of the world, as Donne recognizes that Wotton is ('you may command | Fit matter whether you will write, or doe' 75). To infold, to perplex, the word 'honour' with itself, as in the sixth stanza of 'To Sir Henry Wotton, at his going Ambassador to Venice', is to enact virtue's struggle to clear and maintain its own meaning amid the commonplace approximations, the common practice of men.

If Wotton himself remains a minor poet it is partly because, when he chooses lyric expression, his 'intrinsecal Familiarity' with what men do is not immersed in, is not infused by, the practice of an uncommon alertness to the common practices of speech. In entering even this diffident caveat against the comely verse of 'On his Mistris, the Queen of Bohemia' or the comely prose of Walton's *The Compleat Angler* and *The Life of Sir Henry Wotton* one is liable to be dismissed as some kind of latter-day Ranter or Muggletonian. A style at once so ingenuous and so ingenious appears, indeed, to have taken certain pre-emptive measures against this kind of clownish truculence. Just so, one infers from Mr Asquith's presidential style the solecism that would be committed if one were to so take him at his word ('threadbare amateur') as to treat with scorn his trifling and patronizing 'reflections'. Asquith shows what the tensile seventeenth-century comeliness has been reduced to by 1919, after some three hundred years of drift and occasion and contexture. Wotton's 'You *Common people* of the *Skies*' balances very prettily between political fact and poetical fancy. None the less, viewed in the light of Donne's poem to him, it may appear like an 'example . . . of too great height', self-exempted from Donne's importunate yet humble caveats.

'Fitness', a word of discretion and dispatch ('habilitas'), allowing 'ableness', 'handsomeness', to rub along with compleasance and special pleading, also stands for the maintaining of rectitude. Donne's argument tunes itself into, and against, the word ('Fit matter', 'will to your fortune fit', 'Which fits them', 'nothing else so fit for mee'). These four verse letters show respect not only for Wotton the man but also for the tradition of learned morals, active virtue, which he exemplifies. In addressing his friend Donne undertakes, at a deeper level than convention requires, a rehearsal of the traditional understanding that, by a study of 'the short and sure precepts of good example', a wise man prepared himself to face, unperplexed, the manifold perplexities of state affairs. He goes over what must presently be said and done by going over again what has many times been said and done, and puts himself to school in the very phrases with which he commends ethical scholarship and well-versed moral action:

> But, Sir, I' advise not you, I rather doe
> Say o'er those lessons, which I learn'd of you.
>
> (73)

FOUR

Dryden's Prize-Song

DRYDEN'S lofty contempt for 'common Libellers' (605), his depiction of the 'just' satirist as one 'arm'd with the power of Verse, to Punish and make Examples of the bad' (606), might fairly attract the epithet 'magisterial', compounding as it does the idea of authority and mastery, if it were not for the fact that the poet in his own use of the word hedged it about with various caveats. The 'sublime and daring Genius' of Lucretius, which he likened to that of Hobbes, seemed to him 'Magisterial' in its 'positive assertion' of 'Opinions', its 'disdain' for 'all manner of Replies' (395). He protested that Sir Robert Howard, in his hasty retort upon the essay *Of Dramatick Poesie*, had overlooked the fact that the piece was 'a Dialogue sustain'd by Persons of several Opinions' and had been 'pleased to charge me with being Magisterial' (9: 15). Dryden was concerned that the judicious author, for all his care to establish right meanings, is fated to be misconstrued. 'Many men', he wrote, 'are shock'd at the name of Rules, as if they were a kinde of Magisterial prescription upon Poets' (13: 248). That sentence itself is a confrontation between the hasty 'prejudicate Opinions' (658) of 'many men', those whose 'judgment is a meer Lottery' (17: 73), and his own resolute opinion. Our obligation as informed readers is to take into account both the special pleading and the circumstantial facts, a task made all the more necessary and difficult since Dryden himself draws circumstance ('many men') not only into his critical strategy but also into the timbre of his writing. 'I will first see how this will relish with the Age' (13: 247): he marks down in a word the fickleness of public taste and adds a relish to his own controversial style.

Dr Johnson wrote in his essay on Dryden that 'to judge

rightly of an author, we must transport ourselves to his time, and examine what were the wants of his contemporaries, and what were his means of supplying them'. He added, however, that in such works as the essay *Of Dramatick Poesie* 'the author proves his right of judgement, by his power of performance'. In such a context 'our' capacity to 'judge rightly' of circumstance adumbrates, but is not made equivalent to, the exercise of an author's creative judgement, which is a 'power' that circumstantial considerations neither enhance nor excuse. We have here the makings of an antithesis but Johnson sees that it is a more oblique and complex business than that. Dryden anticipates Johnson's perception. With 'pleased to charge' and 'many men' and 'relish' he 'proves his right of judgement' over the prejudicate and the circumstantial. The dangerous volatile element, present here as it is absent from Johnson's argument, is the contentious special pleading. A sense of injured merit, of what Pound would term the 'intelligence at bay', is strong in Dryden but, like Pound in *The Pisan Cantos*, he seems able to view his own *amour propre* as one among other competing forces in the mundane business; demanding and meriting utterance but also in need of chastening and restraint. Again like Pound he perceives how the thwartness of these things is to be registered 'according to the Etymology of the word' (662). This recognition is manifested not only in the scrupulous anxiety over niceties of translation ('The word *Rejicit* I know will admit of both senses' 1051), but also in the sharpness with which he turns upon one of Howard's solecisms ('*delectus verborum* is no more *Latine* for the Placing of Words, than *Reserate* is *Latine* for shut the Door' 9: 8). In much the same spirit he handles Casaubon's defence of Persius' learning ('he did *ostendere*, but not *ostentare*'), considering that this 'turns it handsomly, upon that supercilious Critick' Scaliger who had accused the Latin poet of ostentatious pedantry (641). 'Turns it handsomly' has its own relish. It sounds like the 'Well done!' that acclaims something at once finely achieved and morally just, where the 'right of judgement' is indeed at one with the 'power of performance' though, in fact, it congratulates one despotic scholar for savaging another. This is a relish which we are to distinguish from the superciliousness of 'taste'.

Dryden's brother-in-law Sir Robert Howard, in taking issue with *Of Dramatick Poesie*, had claimed that "'tis not necessary for Poets to study strict reason' and that 'in the difference of *Tragedy* and *Comedy*, and of *Fars* it self, there can be no determination but by the Taste'. Dryden would have none of this. Such appeals to 'taste' were gestures of surrender not only to the indiscriminate rabble but also to the chaos in the individual mind, 'a confus'd Mass of Thoughts, tumbling over one another in the Dark', which is what inspiration is before its elements are 'either chosen or rejected by the Judgment' (8: 95). 'The liking or disliking of the people gives the Play the denomination of good or bad, but does not really make, or constitute it such' (9: 11). 'Constitute' relates both to the consistency of the thing in itself and to its formal establishment in the public domain. Dryden here differentiates 'denomination' from constitution as emphatically as Ruskin would distinguish between extrinsic and intrinsic value or Pound insist that 'technique is the only gauge and test of a man's lasting sincerity', the instrument by which we distinguish the 'serious artist' from 'the disagreeable young person expressing its haedinus egotism'.

Dryden makes his own concessions, it is true; even in matters of taste and judgement, half-assenting to the polite fiction that on such questions the 'Noblesse' do not share the confusions of 'the multitude, the οἱ πολλοί' (17: 73). But that which is conceded may have been constrained, at best by a sense of obligation, at worst by exaction. The edge of Dryden's arguments is whetted upon this fact. There are 'rules' which are more equitable than 'taste' and there are the requirements of 'compleasance', of 'prejudicate opinions', which confound rules with taste and turn judgement into a parody of itself. When Dryden stresses the necessity for a right 'choice of words' he is, like Pound, emphasizing eloquent cogency ('Our language is noble, full, and significant'; 17: 78, 9: 8) as well as 'propriety of sound' (15: 9). Again like Pound he is opposing the 'graded and measured word' to haedinus egotism; but when Pound claims that 'literature is language charged with meaning' his meaning is more than a little diffused. Quotidian language, both casual and curial, is itself highly charged, but charged with the enormous power of the contingent and circumstantial, a 'confused mass of thoughts', a multitudinous meaning amid which the creative judgement must labour to choose and reject. There are 'meanings' which are self-evidently wrong ('reserate' is not the Latin for 'shut the door') but the 'meaning' of a poem, its constitution, the composition of its elements, is not so readily abstractable from the constituted opinions and solecisms of the age; and though the grading and measuring of words presupposes the ability to recognize ambiguities, there are some ambiguities so deeply impacted with habit, custom, procedure, that the 'recognition' is in effect the acknowledgement of irreducible bafflement. Dryden and Pound are alike in their feeling for a language that is as expressive of the labour and bafflement as it is of the perfected judgement. Sir Robert Howard's kind of 'taste', on the other hand, is the prerogative of a particular kind of confidence, it goes with power and status; and Dryden shares with Montaigne and Bacon a relish for the wry *bon mot* of the philosopher Favorinus chided by his friends for giving way in a dispute with the Emperor on a point of etymology: 'voudriez vous qu'il ne fut pas plus sçavant que moy, luy qui commande à trente legions?'

Bacon alludes to this anecdote in *The Advancement of Learning*: 'Neither was it accounted weakenesse, but discretion in him that would not dispute his best with *Adrianus Caesar*, excusing himselfe, *That it was reason to yeeld to him, that commaunded thirtie Legions.* These and the like applications and stooping to points of necessitie and conuenience cannot bee disallowed.' The way the question is put, both in Montaigne's French and in Florio's English version of it, the curt confrontation of 'you', 'him', and 'I' discreetly rendered in the routine civility 'voudriez vous', *'would you not have him to be much wiser then I'*, is only partly glossed by Bacon's 'stooping to . . . necessitie and conuenience'. The sardonic conflation of the fiction of free choice with the fact of *force majeure* is not precisely the same as an equation in Machiavellian diplomacy. One may indeed state with exemplary frankness the 'reasons' for an unavoidable avoidance of absolute frankness in dealings with the world of power and prerogative. Dryden, who was well acquainted with Montaigne's essays, alludes to the same riposte, both in *A Defence of an Essay of Dramatick Poesy* and in his preface to *All for Love*. What Bacon calls 'discretion' he dubs 'good grace' in those who had 'Wit enough to yield the Prize . . . and not contend with him who had thirty Legions: They were sure to be rewarded if they confess'd themselves bad Writers, and that was somewhat better than to be Martyrs for their reputation' (13: 15). Dryden's irony is the more strained and the words 'wit enough' and 'good grace' exacerbate that tone. In the preface to his translation of Ovid's *Epistles* he writes 'But Deeds, it seems, may be Justified by Arbitrary Power, when words are question'd in a Poet' (178). Taken together, Dryden's 'justified by Arbitrary Power . . .' and Johnson's '. . . proves his right of judgement, by his power of performance', statements too much at odds to be resolved by a formal oxymoron or paradox, mark out an area of bafflement, stultification, which the creative intelligence is forced to encounter as though it possessed the 'brute' force that C. S. Peirce imputes to 'actuality'. 'Style', whether regarded as a series of tactical accommodations along the lines of Boileau's *L'Art poétique* or as 'nothing short of a desperate ontological or metaphysical manœuvre', must in some form admit the contrary of that which it affirms. It is undoubtedly true that the French seventeenth-century neo-classicists propounded 'the necessity for rendering the action [of a play] conformable to the particular taste of the audience' but even in that critical description the words 'necessity', 'conformable', 'particular taste' bristle with Hobbesian contradictions. Behind Boileau's trim prescriptive questions ('Voulez-vous du public meriter les amours?', 'Voulez-vous sur la scene étaler des ouvrages . . .?', 'Voulez-vous longtemps plaire, et jamais ne lasser?', 'Voulez-vous faire aimer vos riches fictions?') stands the question of Montaigne's Favorinus 'voudriez vous qu'il ne fut pas plus sçavant que moy, luy qui commande à trente legions?'

To the suggestion that such a conclusion is merely impressionistic I would answer that the actual writings of the French theorists strongly qualify Joel Spingarn's notion of the 'single point of view' which, in his estimation, particularly recommended them to English authors and audiences 'eager for the results rather than the processes of such discussion'. There may be, in Boileau, d'Aubignac, and others, a final emphasis but that is not at all the same thing as a single point of view. D'Aubignac's emphasis, in his *Pratique du théâtre*, is in fact divided between imperative advice that the poet-dramatist should render his work 'admirable aux Spectateurs: car il ne travaille que pour leur plaire' and the equal imperative to contrive everything 'comme s'il n'y avoit point de Spectateurs'. So too Dryden divides his emphasis when in *The Dedication of the Aeneis* he writes 'A Poet cannot speak too plainly on the Stage: for *Volat irrevocabile verbum*; the sense is lost if it be not taken flying: but what we read alone we have leisure to digest. There an Author may beautifie his Sense by the boldness of his Expression, which if we understand not fully at the first, we may dwell upon it, 'till we find the secret force and excellence' (1010). Such statements excite awkward questions. Of what purpose or value is it to arouse the admiration and good will of your audience if, in the act of catering to their tastes and prejudice, you must forgo 'the secret force and excellence' of the work? We seem here to brush against the prejudice that stage business is too conversant with mundane opinion, 'compleasance', '*negotium*', a more superficial exercise than is that 'dwelling upon' the matter which only solitary 'leisure' can give.

Such an emphasis would not be alien to the aloof humanism of Montaigne, admired by English writers of the period from Bacon to Dryden and by none more keenly than by those whose circumstances forced them to confront the tyranny of the market-place. 'La tourbe, mere d'ignorance, d'injustice et d'inconstance.' Those lines in Dryden's 'The Medall' beginning 'Almighty Crowd, thou shorten'st all dispute' (256) read like a close paraphrase of Montaigne's opinion. Viewed from a different angle, Montaigne's disdainful emphasis on 'facile' in 'au peuple, juge peu exacte, facile à piper, facile à contenter' satirically pre-empts the advice of Boileau and others as to the desirability of ease and facility in one's striving for public success: 'N'offrez rien au Lecteur que ce qui peut luy plaire.'

Montaigne, it must be added, had, from the age of thirty-eight when he took possession of his little castle, the library on the third floor of the round tower, sufficient means to hold himself aloof, physically and spiritually, from 'la tourbe'. Dryden, despite the fact that he came of a landowning family and had married an earl's daughter, did not enjoy such freedom. In the idiom of the day both Montaigne and he could be said to 'drive' their 'studies' to the end of private and public improvement; but Dryden was also driven by what he called 'the Vocation of Poverty to scribble' (13: 14). Montaigne, contemplating his own position of vantage, mused on 'le monde' and 'moy': 'Les autres vont tousjours ailleurs, s'ils y pensent bien; ils vont tousjours avant . . . moy je me roulle en moy mesme.' Dryden was one who had necessarily to go 'tousjours avant'; there was no option. He contracted with the Theatre Royal, *c.*1668, 'to write three plays annually in return for one and a quarter shares', a contract which he never managed fully to honour. In the last years of his life his business dealings with the publisher Tonson, closely calculated on both sides, which certainly promised profitable returns, rendered him accountable to his partner for every line; and that is a rather different thing from making oneself accountable for every word. Montaigne, from the age of thirty-eight, was at liberty to meditate at his choice and desire. Dryden knew that there were liberties which he could not afford to take or would take at his peril. We weigh "tis dangerous to offend an Arbitrary Master' (1020) against 'When a Poet is throughly provok'd, he will do himself Justice, however dear it cost him' (1016) and conclude that Dryden's own style is a matter of constant vigilant negotiation among and between 'danger', 'justice', and 'cost'. It may be added that it is one of the virtues of his style to transform a driven condition into a cadenced vehemence and that 'however dear it cost him' strikes one as having earned its place in the syntax of his conviction as Montaigne's 's'ils y pensent bien' does not. On the other hand, when Dryden in a letter of 1673 compliments the Earl of Rochester on possessing 'all the happinesse of an idle life, join'd with the good Nature of an Active' (Ls 9), he is, by implication, acknowledging the weight and import of Montaigne's 'moy je me roulle en moy mesme'. Even for the most public, the most 'occasional', of poets his outgoing energy must reciprocally depend on the degree to which he can roll him into himself; and Dryden shows that he is not unaware of the extent to which 'a flood of little businesses, which yet are necessary to . . . Subsistance' (Ls 123) imposes a ceaseless attrition upon this intimate creative selfhood. The fact that, year in year out, he transcended his circumstances in his art does not diminish the force of the observation. In the end he sent the publisher of the *Fables* more than eleven thousand lines instead of the ten thousand for which he had contracted. This is what is referred to, rather too easily, as his giving 'good measure'. Dryden gave good measure in the structure and cadence of his lines and paragraphs where '*otium*' and '*nec-otium*' come together in the only way that counts. There is nothing in his own theorizing to suggest that he would dissent from Boileau's 'Que toûjours le Bon sens s'accorde avec la Rime' but in his practice he contrives his 'harmony' ('Verse . . . or . . . the other Harmony of Prose' 1446) not only out of the 'natural Disadvantages, the 'Monosyllables' of English 'clog'd with consonants' (13: 223; see also 1053), the laborious negotiating of 'le bon sens' amid the heavy-laden language of 'custom and common use' (17: 29), but also out of a reconciling of circumstance and judgement not unlike that 'daily practice in the World' of a statesman whom he admired and praised: his capacity 'to work and bend [men's] stubborn Minds, which go not all after the same Grain, but each of them so particular a way, that the same common Humours, in several Persons, must be wrought upon by several Means' (8: 97). One hears from time to time of Dryden's 'duplicity', 'ambivalence', 'doubletalk', and 'shuffling'. I do not think one can so describe a man at bay without observing an ambivalence within the term 'at bay' itself. It is both 'the chorus of barking raised by hounds in immediate conflict with a hunted animal' and the 'position of a hunted animal when, unable to flee farther, it turns, faces the hounds, and defends itself at close quarters'. The 'chorus' determines the 'position' but the creature in that position manifests its own determination and may well force the chorus back upon an urgent and surprising redefinition.

When Dryden, in the preface to *All for Love*, refers contemptuously to 'this Rhyming Judge of the Twelvepenny

Gallery' (13: 17) he is retorting upon an attack by the Earl of Rochester. He affects to believe that his assailant is one of the 'Petits Esprits' rather than someone whose status as one 'of the highest Rank, and truest Understanding' (1052–3) it would be dangerous to deny; Dryden dismisses a man whose social prerogative is to dismiss others. With a throw-away colloquialism he precisely infringes a set of aesthetic distinctions based on social hierarchy. Jean Segrais divided literary critics into three classes and Dryden followed his lead in the *Dedication of the Aeneis*: beginning with the 'Mobb-Readers', moving to 'a middle sort' unable to discern the difference between 'ostentatious Sentences, and the true sublime', and ending with 'the Highest Court of Judicature, like that of the Peers', of which, Dryden adds, his dedicatee the Earl of Mulgrave 'is so great an Ornament' (1052–3). Our contemporary scepticism fastens upon Dryden's own ostentatious and placatory sentences in his addresses to patrons; his own scepticism, working a more dangerous track, implies that 'Mobb-Readers' are to be found at all levels, including that of the patrons. In his *Discourse concerning the Original and Progress of Satire* he concedes that one of the reasons for the obscurity of Aulus Persius Flaccus in his satires may have been that 'the fear of his safety under *Nero*, compell'd him to this darkness in some places' (639). It is reasonable to suppose that anything written as code will be 'obscure'. Dryden's insult to Rochester, though in code, could not be more clear. For 'rhyming judge of the twelvepenny gallery' we are to read 'one who purports to belong to "the highest court of judicature" ' and, further, 'one who commands thirty legions'. The deliberated insult has the quality of impenetrable transparency. In the *Dedication of Examen Poeticum* Dryden sketches the circumstances that require and provoke this kind of disingenuous ingenuousness: 'If I am the Man, as I have Reason to believe, who am seemingly Courted, and secretly Undermin'd: I think I shall be able to defend my self, when I am openly Attacqu'd' (793). To be 'seemingly courted', 'secretly undermined', implies that 'strife' is cynically accommodated to 'the Politeness of *Rome*' (661). It also means that courtship and treachery are accommodated to each other. The 'openness' of 'I think I shall be able to defend my self, when I am openly Attacqu'd' suggests that the massive plainness of Dryden is a very different thing from 'the plain style' as it is commonly conceived and that it has more in common with Davenant's argument when, directly calling upon the tutelary spirit of Hobbes, he likens the poet's progress amid 'the Learned' to one who 'travails through the Enemy's country' and the 'wise Poet' to 'a wise Generall' who 'will not shew his strengths till they are in exact government and order; which are not the postures of chance, but proceed from Vigilance and labour'.

What *Virgil* wrote in the vigour of his Age, in Plenty and at Ease, I have undertaken to *Translate* in my Declining Years: strugling with Wants, oppress'd with Sickness, curb'd in my Genius, lyable to be misconstrued in all I write; and my Judges, if they are not very equitable, already prejudic'd against me, by the *Lying Character* which has been given them of my Morals. Yet steady to my Principles, and not dispirited with my Afflictions, I have, by the Blessing of God on my Endeavours, overcome all difficulties; and, in some measure, acquitted my self of the Debt which I ow'd the Publick, when I undertook this Work. (1424)

The strength of Dryden's own argument stems here from its being at once ingenuous and at bay. While genuinely striving to accommodate itself to a style of compleasant address (it is from the 'Postscript to the Reader' of the *Aeneis* translation) it is imbued with resentment against those 'curbs' and 'misconstruc- tions' which are the inevitable dark side of 'civility and affability'. Dryden is careful to establish and confirm an unambitious contractual tone with 'undertaken', 'undertook', 'Endeavours', 'acquitted'. The more ambitiously emotive words, 'strugling', 'oppress'd', 'curb'd', are both restrained and justified by the unemotional. The unemotional is part of the emotive, as plainness has its part to play in eloquence. We are not able, we are not invited, to distinguish precisely between the elements of sober factual recital, bitter special pleading, righteous indignation, wounded *amour propre*. Dryden's tone persuades us that though the injustices may be cogently summarized they are not to be summarily passed over. The 'Publick' is in debt to him for all those injuries received, even though with overt modesty he acknowledges that 'Debt which I ow'd the Publick, when I undertook this Work'. This passage, written near the end of his life, is a summation of those several utterances of endurance, indignation, and honest doubt heard at intervals throughout his work: the theatre prologues and epilogues, the critical essays, the dedications. "'Tis not that I am mortified to all ambition, but I scorn as much to take it from half-witted Judges, as I shou'd to raise an Estate by cheating of Bubbles'; 'For the Reputation . . . of my Poetry, it shall either stand by its own Merit; or fall for want of it' (791). It is also, by implication, the résumé of a long history of 'prejudic'd' 'misconstruing'; of Rochester's accusations of arrogance and Shadwell's sneers. In such passages of self-vindication style itself turns 'at bay'. When, in the *Discourse Concerning Satire*, Dryden rehearses the real and alleged defects of style in the work of Aulus Persius Flaccus, its metrical lameness, the crowded obscurity of its diction, one senses not only his own constrained adherence to compleasance—it is 'stubborn, insociable, froward, intractable' to write like that— but also the strong pull of sympathy towards that very stubbornness and intractability. I am here thinking less of the appeals to mitigating circumstances (Persius wrote in the days of Nero, he died before he had arrived at maturity of judgement) than of the qualified but distinct admiration for the exacerbated, as well as the exacerbating, spirit of such work. Dryden the theorist would no doubt urge a distinction between raw power and a deliberated 'boldness of . . . Expression' that may be dwelt upon at leisure "till we find the secret force and excellence'; in practice, as in the elegy 'To the Memory of Mr. Oldham', he comes close to compounding the two. There is something secreted in his praise of such 'secret force', a judgement that eludes and transcends the immediate circumstance. It is the 'prevailing character or spirit', the 'characteristic method or procedure', of the work, its 'genius' according to contemporary terminology; but it is also a superior power bestowed, as though by 'the Blessing of God', on the 'Endeavour' itself, on that creative spirit which turns at bay upon the compleasant maxims of the age; it becomes that 'Genius' which enables a poem to 'force its own reception in the World' (215). Eliot is quite wrong in his contention that Dryden's words 'state immensely, but their suggestiveness is almost nothing', that they lack 'overtone' or 'nebula'; and Auden is, to say the least, rash when he claims that 'they mean exactly what, on first reading, they seem to say'.

> Farewel, too little and too lately known,
> Whom I began to think and call my own;
> For sure our Souls were near ally'd; and thine
> Cast in the same Poetick mould with mine.
> One common Note on either Lyre did strike,
> And Knaves and Fools we both abhorr'd alike:
> To the same Goal did both our Studies drive,
> The last set out the soonest did arrive.
> Thus *Nisus* fell upon the slippery place,
> While his young Friend perform'd and won the Race.
> O early ripe! to thy abundant store
> What could advancing Age have added more?
> It might (what Nature never gives the young)
> Have taught the numbers of thy native Tongue.
> But Satyr needs not those, and Wit will shine
> Through the harsh cadence of a rugged line.
> A noble Error, and but seldom made,
> When Poets are by too much force betray'd.
> Thy generous fruits, though gather'd ere their prime
> Still shew'd a quickness; and maturing time
> But mellows what we write to the dull sweets of Rime.
> Once more, hail and farewel; farewel thou young,
> But ah too short, *Marcellus* of our Tongue;
> Thy Brows with Ivy, and with Laurels bound;
> But Fate and gloomy Night encompass thee around.

(389)

'To the Memory of Mr. Oldham' was Dryden's contribution to a set of memorial verses prefacing the *Remains of Mr. John Oldham in Verse and Prose*, 1684. It is a poem that contrives to be harmonious and generous in recollection while exercising discernment in its weighing of virtues and limitations and of what, in the circumstances, one is free to say of these. It harmonizes with the general tenor of lament and tribute. One of Dryden's fellow memorialists, in an anonymous contribution, also likens Oldham to Marcellus. Dryden's piece recollects in style, and the style is judiciously reminiscent of the spirit in which Oldham himself had composed 'To the Memory . . . of Mr. Charles Morwent', 'To the Memory of . . . Mr. Harman Atwood', 'Upon the Works of Ben Johnson', and 'A Satyr Touching Nobility | Out of Monsieur Boileau'. In Oldham's elegies for friends, a 'blooming Ripeness' and 'full ripe Vertues' are fancied as eternized even in their untimely cropping, in the fashion of Horatian paradox; and the dead man is spared 'dull Habitude'. Ben Jonson is lauded by Oldham as 'Rich in thy self, to whose unbounded store | Exhausted Nature could vouchsafe no more', and the words 'A Fool, or Knave' occur in the 'Satyr touching Nobility'.

In November 1684, when 'To the Memory of Mr. Oldham' first appeared, Dryden was in his fifty-fourth year and had been Poet Laureate for well over a decade. Oldham had died in 1683, aged thirty. His life had been the common career of impecunious drudgery until, shortly before his death, 'he was taken into [the] Patronage' of the Earl of Kingston and 'lived with him in great respect at *Holme-Pierpont* in *Nottinghamshire*'. He had also attracted, and unlike Dryden had not lost, the favour of the Earl of Rochester. It has been suggested that 1684 was a 'relatively serene' year in Dryden's life. Compared with the previous two years it may have been relatively free from vituperation and libel but to suppose it in any way 'serene' is to underrate the power of memory and its capacity to affect current thoughts and emotions. 'Memory' was for Dryden a creative faculty. Sixteen years later, in the Preface to the *Fables*, he would speak of himself as being 'as vigorous as ever in the Faculties of my Soul, excepting only my Memory, which is not impair'd to any great degree' (1446). The poem to Oldham is an 'in memoriam' where the formal commitment to recollection, embodied in the virtually seamless texture of literary echoes, touches upon actual and urgent memories, both overt and tacit; the overt being taken up with the commemoration of a common cause against 'Knaves and Fools' and the tacit, not unrelated to that cause, gravitating to thoughts of ill luck and ill usage: thoughts with which the remembrance of Oldham is perplexingly implicated.

It has been said that Rochester's 'capricious patronage of poets brought in its train envy, backbiting and hatred'. Dryden had

Chapter Four

fallen from favour around the year 1675 and Rochester's attack on him was circulating, anonymously, shortly afterwards. At about the same time Oldham was received into favour. Not only did the younger man supplant Dryden in the esteem of a powerful and dangerous coterie; he may also be said to have pre-empted the elder poet's claim to be regarded as the innovator of heroic satire. Oldham's *Satyrs upon the Jesuits*, which established his celebrity, was published in 1680–1, the year before *Absalom and Achitophel*, but Dryden's *MacFlecknoe*, which is a strange hybrid, a heroic lampoon, was circulating in manuscript probably some three years before Oldham's satires were written and five years before they appeared in print. 'A transcript of part of [*MacFlecknoe*] in Oldham's hand . . . is dated "Aº 1678" ' (1914) and other poets borrowed from it before it was published in 1682. Dryden's succinct adaptation, in the 'Oldham' elegy, of the foot-race episode from Book V of the *Aeneid* reads like an open verdict on these circumstances. In Virgil's rendering of the scene the Trojan contest is scarcely an exercise in simple-hearted virtue and magnanimity. It is marred by several instances of unsportsmanlike behaviour and complaint, like 'disagreeable young person[s] expressing [their] haedinus egotism', and terminates in the wholesale distribution of handsome consolation-prizes that take the edge off victory and the sting from defeat. None of this is lost in Dryden's version. Euryalus, the victor, is awarded 'a stately Steed' (1182) but Nisus comes off very handsomely with 'an ample Shield; | Of wond'rous Art by *Didymaon* wrought' (1184). One wonders whether this is a display of civic equity, 'equal Justice' or of aesthetic anarchy: 'Then thus the Prince; let no Disputes arise: | Where Fortune plac'd it, I award the Prize. | But Fortune's Errors give me leave to mend, | At least to pity my deserving Friend' (1183). This may be the 'indulgent' face of patronage, a master-stroke of magisterial aplomb; but Aeneas still reminds one of Sir Robert Howard proclaiming that 'in the difference of *Tragedy* and *Comedy*, and of *Fars* it self, there can be no determination but by the *Taste*'. 'To the Memory of Mr. Oldham' is Dryden's 'Shield' and 'wond'rous Art', his consolation, his own prize-song. Its art is demonstrated by the stylishness with which it both maintains

76

the decorum of 'indulgence' and implies the cost that decorum extorts from 'curb'd' genius. 'Thus *Nisus* fell . . .' The Latin of Book V has 'sed . . .'. Dryden contrives to blend into the echoes of Book V the heartfelt panegyric ('venerande puer', 'fortunati ambo!') and the heroic sorrow of Book IX, in which Euryalus and Nisus fall in battle, race together into death. Such a tone is much more appropriate for a funeral elegy, as is the last line's invocation of Book VI ('sed nox atra caput tristi circumvolat umbra'). The 'wonder' is that, beneath it, runs a contrary thread, as though Dryden were sardonically taking Howard at his word and as though there were indeed '*no difference betwixt* Comedy *and* Tragedy *but what is made by the taste only*' (9: 11). 'Thus *Nisus* fell upon the slippery place . . .' 'Slippery place' suggests a Senecan sententiousness but is discreetly adapting 'sed pronus in ipso | concidit immundoque fimo sacroque cruore'. 'Fimus' is animal excrement. Nisus slips in the dung and blood of the freshly sacrificed animals. Our own coarse colloquialism 'in the shit', apparently not current before the mid-nineteenth century, might fairly describe Dryden's feeling about the general run of his worldly luck; but 'Thus *Nisus* fell upon the slippery place', which slides together some five lines of the source, manages to be both euphemistic and decently 'classical'. 'His Heels flew up; and on the grassy Floor, | He fell, besmear'd with Filth, and Holy Gore' (1182) is how Dryden pitches it in his *Aeneis*. 'His Heels flew up' could be from a ballad of low life. The cleaned-up phrasing of the 'Oldham' elegy does not completely disguise, however, the indecencies of the world's ill luck, inequitable, 'indulgent' judgements, and outrageous juxta-positions. The *victor ludorum* prize for which, through the ludicrous collapse of Nisus, Euryalus unexpectedly qualifies is at once the 'stately Steed' of poetic acclaim and an early death.

One senses, at the same time, that Dryden disdains to write for Oldham an 'Insolent, Sparing, and Invidious Panegyrick' (603) and that this refusal is as much a matter of self-respect as of respect for the subject. Sincerity is a complex, not a simple, state. If poetry were simply plain statement, discourse, one would conclude that Dryden is several times unjust not only to his own superior qualities as a poet but also to the power and accuracy of his own critical judgement. 'A noble Error, and but seldom made, | When Poets are by too much force betray'd.' Oldham himself is something of a special pleader on the matter, acknowledging that 'some persons found fault with the rough-ness of my Satyrs formerly publisht' but contending that 'the way I took, was out of choice, not want of judgment' and that 'I did not so much mind the Cadence, as the Sense and expressiveness of my words, and therefore chose not those, which were best dispos'd to placing themselves in Rhyme, but rather the most keen, and tuant, as being the suitablest to my Argument'. Robert Gould, in 'To the Memory of Mr. John Oldham', follows suit with 'How wide shoot they, that strive to blast thy Fame, | By saying, that thy Verse was rough and lame?' and with the further suggestion that such critics misconstrue the function and style of satire by asking it to produce the same effect as 'plyant' and 'smooth' love verses. Gould's tribute was not included in the first edition of the *Remains*; it was added in 1687, the same year in which his attack on Dryden—*The Laureat . . . Jack Squob's History . . .*—appeared in print. It is possible, therefore, that Gould is 'shooting' at Dryden in his defence of Oldham, bridling at those graciously measured reservations as if they had been attempts to 'blast' Oldham's reputation. Such pleas beg the question that Dryden would be least inclined to indulge or overlook: the question of how far 'Sense and expressiveness' can be accomplished where 'Cadence' is not minded. I concur with the view that Dryden's poem, while demonstrating magnanimity of judgement in this matter of opinion, teaches a strict lesson in how to master sense and expressiveness through cadence and rhyme. The main burden of his statement is critical and prosodic but there is sufficient 'nebula' to blur criticism into notions of high vocation and salutary sternness. It is helpful, in the circumstances, that both 'rugged' and 'harsh' permit a latitude of interpretation. They could be taken to mean either technical inadequacy, or the possession of a stalwart, independent virtue, or the 'true end of Satyre . . . the amendment of Vices by correction' (216). Dryden referred at various times to a 'rugged, and unharmonious' verse of ten monosyllables (1054), of which there are numerous instances in Oldham's work, to 'the plainness, fierceness, rugged virtue | Of an old true-stamp *Roman*' (13: 27), and to the need for satire to prescribe 'harsh Remedies to an inveterate Disease' (216). When he claims on Oldham's behalf that 'Wit will shine | Through the harsh cadence of a rugged line' the sonorities of plain statement are diffused into a number of overtones. Such words do not directly consent to the special pleading but neither do they directly rebuke it. Dryden is engaged not only with the combined weight of social expectation and literary convention, and with his genuine liking and sympathy for the younger man, but also with the knowledge of his own extreme vulnerability to the kind of partisan mis-construing that men like Robert Gould were so ready to make.

In the *Discourse concerning the Original and Progress of Satire*, published some eight years after the 'Oldham' elegy, Dryden commemorates the achievement, and observes the faults, of the Roman poets Lucan and Persius. His reluctance to charge them with 'Faults, from which Humane Nature, and more especially in Youth, can never possibly be exempted' is matched by his readiness to 'wonder how they, who Dyed before the Thirtieth Year of their Age, cou'd write so well, and think so strongly' (640). Oldham was just thirty when he died:

> Thy generous fruits, though gather'd ere their prime
> Still shew'd a quickness; and maturing time
> But mellows what we write to the dull sweets of Rime. ⎫
> ⎬
> ⎭

'We' is again concessionary; it condescends, in the sense then prevailing: it stoops voluntarily and graciously; but condescension and compleasance are bound into the same nexus. 'Rime', like cadence, is for Dryden the means whereby the poet achieves 'sense and expressiveness'. 'Dull sweets of Rime' submits judgement to circumstance rather as Dryden exempts noble patrons from 'Faults, from which Humane Nature', one might reasonably think, 'can never possibly be exempted'. In verses written at about the same time as the 'Oldham' elegy and addressed 'To the Earl of *Roscomon*, on his Excellent *Essay* on *Translated Verse*', rhyme as 'Manly Sweetness' in the right hands (e.g. Roscommon's) is contrasted with its debasing effect in the

wrong hands (the French): 'At best a pleasing Sound, and fair
barbarity' (387). The personal note in 'To the Memory of
Mr. Oldham' is intense, but not so simplistically that we are
obliged to see Dryden fearing his own inevitable decline into
mellifluous etiolation. The triple rhyme and alexandrine, enforcing
our awareness of 'rime' even as he condescends to dismiss its
'dull sweets', make a triple *congé* to language, judgement and
circumstance; to the various enforcements and agreements of
'Civil Conversation' (648) and to what 'wond'rous Art' can
make of them.

Bunyan's Mr By-ends makes 'a very low *Conje*, and they also
gave him a *Complement*', 'they' being Mr *Hold-the-World*,
Mr *Mony-love*, and Mr *Save-all*. Dryden anticipates Bunyan in
a poem of 1677: 'For ill Men, conscious of their inward guilt, |
Think the best Actions on By-ends are built' (162). We are some
way towards appreciating the genius with which Dryden drives
his trade when we recognize that, for him, those acquaintances
of Bunyan's By-ends, and other cruel and meretricious figures
of striving Restoration 'compleasance'—'my Lord *Turn-about*,
my Lord *Time-server*, my Lord *Fair-speech* . . . Also Mr. *Smooth-
man*, Mr. *Facing-bothways*, Mr. *Any-thing*'—are to be encountered
in the *otium* and *negotium*, the self-elected exemptions and the
'little businesses . . . necessary to . . . Subsistance', that
constitute the art itself and the criticism which attends, patronizes,
and reduces it to order: ''tis dangerous to offend an Arbitrary
Master.' Good writing is a contributor to 'Civil Conversation',
yet at the same time it is not; it 'travails through the Enemy's
country' along the paths of civil conversation and 'the common
Track of Business, which is not always clean' (915). That
common track is less a cheerily nid-nodding consensus than a
treadmill of progress ('ils vont tousjours avant') where many
incompatibles are obliged to keep some semblance of common
time and order. What we call the writer's 'distinctive voice' is a
registering of different voices. It is because those exemplary
names in *The Pilgrim's Progress* ('Mr. *Smooth-man*'; 'Mr. *Any-
thing*') combine both the fierceness of Bunyan's contempt and
the relish of his well-rewarded vigilance, and because he urges
them forward upon the 'track of business' by his innate sense of

rhythm and cadence, that they lodge themselves so in our minds, coming up out of the common stock and yet newly created with a fresh distinction, which is the only distinction proper to a writer.

'Distinction' may also be conferred as a matter of status by public fiat, *force majeure*, corporate obtuseness, or political expediency, like the laureateships conferred on Thomas Shadwell, Henry James Pye, and Alfred Austin, or like the accolade 'good writing' itself. Such absurdities may with some justice be recorded by an expletive (*'merde alors!'*) because such an expletive doubly satisfies our sense of the arbitrary. At a primitive level it too is an expression of 'intelligence at bay'. The 'prosaic' strength that poetry must have, that sense of being 'loaded with life', the virtue of being 'good sense, at all events', requires, I would say, that the implications of 'at all events' are not readily separable from the implications of '. . . *alors*' ('at that time', 'in that case', 'well, then', 'so what'). Even in those sentences that sound most at bay (Wyatt's 'what thynge is that that these mene wolde not wreste for there purpose that wreste suche thynges', Pound's 'In the gloom, the gold gathers the light against it') there is the particular force and relish of an 'exact government and order; which are not the postures of chance, but proceed from Vigilance and labour'. Style is a seamless contexture of energy and order which, time after time, the effete and the crass somehow contrive to part between them; either paying tremulous lip-service to the 'incomparable' and the 'incommunicable' or else toadying to some current notion of the demotic.

Pound observed in a late interview that 'a great deal of literature is born of hate and . . . whatever is sound in it emerges from the ruins'; and Dryden's contemporary, Samuel Butler, noted in his commonplace book that 'Malice' has 'Power . . . above all other Passions, to highten Wit and Fancy', adding that 'Panegyriques' are 'commonly as Dull as they are false'. 'To the Memory of Mr. Oldham' is a 'panegyrique' which seeks to be lively and true and to associate with magnanimity those qualities of wit and fancy which Butler saw as the prerogative of malice. Dryden's strength and integrity manifest themselves in his running the difficult middle course between the impositions and implications of 'Voulez-vous du public meriter les amours?' and 'voudriez vous qu'il ne fut pas plus sçavant que moy, luy qui commande à trente legions?' One does not break decorum, or even syntax, in shifting from the *bienséance* of the first to the cynical stoicism of the second. Dryden does not break decorum either; for decorum becomes magnanimity, while magnanimity does not annul the force of his own feelings. 'When a Poet is throughly provok'd, he will do himself Justice, however dear it cost him.' When the poet has been 'provok'd' into magnanimity we should not, in justice, underrate the cost of that.

FIVE

'Envoi (1919)'

'ENVOI (1919)' recalls in its title the form of the alba (e.g. 'Alba Innominata', a version of which Pound had included in his *Exultations* of 1909) and in its opening lines the melody of Waller's 'Go lovely Rose' which had been set by Milton's friend and collaborator, the Royalist musician Henry Lawes. From the time of his first discovery of Lawes's music Pound held it in the highest esteem. 'To Thomas Campion his ghost, and to the ghost of Henry Lawes, as prayer for the revival of music': so runs the dedication to the translation of Cavalcanti's 'Donna mi prega' which Pound published in 1928. It is equally the case that Pound held the theory and practice of the nineteenth-century French poet Théophile Gautier, particularly his *Émaux et Camées*, in comparably high esteem and that Gautier's prescriptive 'Chaque pièce devait être un médaillon . . .' can be seen as anticipating the title of 'Medallion', the final poem in *Hugh Selwyn Mauberley*. At the same time, as Pound suggested in an essay of February 1918, 'On the Hard and Soft in French Poetry', to view 'hardness' itself as 'a virtue in the poetic' is an error; the hardness must be a virtue in the 'intent'; the poet should be 'intent on conveying a certain verity of feeling'. Gautier, according to Pound, understood this; Heredia, 'perhaps the best' of his followers, did not. Among the English poets of the generation immediately preceding his own Pound singled out Lionel Johnson as one with 'similar ambitions' to Gautier, adding that 'if Gautier had not written, Johnson's work might even take its place in Welt-literatur . . . might stand for this clearness and neatness'. Those careful locutions ('if Gautier had not written', 'might even take its place') sufficiently temper the enthusiasm and provide circumstantial evidence for those who

would retain 'Medallion' as a poem by the fictional Hugh
Selwyn Mauberley rather than as a lyric by E. P. The principles
are 'hard' but the practice, which shapes the final cameo,
celebrates a 'virtue in the poetic' rather than in the intent. 'The
eyes turn topaz.' We are invited to observe a quality where we
might have expected to receive 'a certain verity of feeling'.

All this adds up to what anxious scholarship describes as an
'interpretative crisis'. Up to a point the scholar's desire for terra
firma is analogous, though not equivalent, to the poet's search
for a 'strategic position' and Pound, the scholar-poet, would not
be unsympathetic to a desire for precise definition hard-won
from those perplexities of circumstance which Henri Gaudier
had called 'the incessant struggle in the complex city'. But it
would be sentimental to claim too close a rapport on this basis.
To complain that a critical reading which differs from one's own
'destroys the only planned structure discernible in *HSM*' is to
sound like someone whose fractious child has just knocked the
jigsaw off the table; and to argue that 'Part II of *Mauberley* is in
general more satisfactory than Part I: we are surer of the object
that Pound has his eye on' is in effect, if not in intention, to
reverse the order of priorities upon which he always insisted.
When Pound wrote, in 1910, 'Villon is no theorist, he is an
objective fact' he was not encouraging us to impose critical
theories about the primacy of objective fact upon our reading of
poetic artefacts. Criticism which is, on many occasions, the
faculty and instrument of judgement is on other occasions,
possibly more numerous, part of the body of circumstance out
of which and against which the single voice of creative
intelligence must be made articulate. Modern criticism in this
guise is one of the shapes of protean Opinion, one of the petty
'lords of the temporal world', something quite other than that
'sublimity of the critical sense' which Pound associated with
Henry James at his strongest. *Homage to Sextus Propertius* and
Hugh Selwyn Mauberley are noteworthy for the manner in which
Opinion not only as the prejudiced voice but also as the pre-
judging ear, figures among the dramatis personae of the work,
and for the way in which 'sublimity of the critical sense' is kept
resolutely in view amid the clamour and the 'gross silence'.

Pound suggested as much when he remarked that 'Mauberley is
. . . an attempt to condense the James novel' since he was contend-
ing in 1918 that though James at his weakest offers a mere '*étude* in
ephemera' at his best he does, nevertheless, treat of major forces,
even of epic forces, and in a way all his own'. To anyone inclined
to suggest that my emphasis on 'the body of circumstance' is
ludicrously out of proportion to Pound's 'major forces' I would
respond that, in 'the domination of modern life', it is the
'ephemera', 'all sorts of intangible bondage', that have usurped
the role of the ancient epic forces and that Pound is at least the
equal of Ben Jonson and Dryden, both in recognizing this factor
and in discovering how to treat of it 'in a way all his own'.

Pound's criticism, particularly of those he most admired,
concentrates attention upon the forces of attrition, upon the
resistant virtues of morale and style, and upon those flaws, even
in the best, which helplessly collude with the ruling imbecilities.
He said 'I am tired of hearing pettiness talked about Henry
James's style.' His own view and sense of style are 'epic'.
Subsumed in this, 'pettiness', 'ephemera', have their ponderable
mass and weight. Whitman, he says, 'goes bail for the nation':
an epic tribute; yet he argued that Whitman was badly flawed
and hampered by his 'catalogues and flounderings', his 'crudity'.
Indebted as Pound was to Laurence Binyon's *The Flight of the
Dragon* (1911), and to his conversation, he none the less deplored
Binyon's 'disgusting attitude of respect toward predecessors
whose intellect is vastly inferior to his own'. Influenced in his
own thinking by Allen Upward's *The Divine Mystery*, which, in
1913, he described as 'the most fascinating book on folk-lore
that I have ever opened', and by the same author's *The New
Word*, he could bring himself to suggest, after Upward's suicide,
that he had 'shot himself in discouragement on reading of [the
Nobel] award to Shaw. Feeling of utter hopelessness in struggle
for values.' Such a timbre is not unlike Upward's own in his
autobiography, which has been defined as one of 'forced levity
and grim desperation . . . betraying the lacerated spirit'. Even
so, Upward remained for Pound 'the old combattant' and is so
commemorated in the first of *The Pisan Cantos*. Such sweeping
disparities in fact stem from a coherent emphasis: that the

self-same writer may become the helpless and hopeless victim of those circumstances which he has acutely diagnosed and assayed. This is to view the matter in its most negative aspect. One can concede the perplexity more positively in the words which Pound used when reviewing the life's work, the interlocked strengths and weaknesses, of A. R. Orage: 'you could call [him] a damn fool *and* respect him.' There remains an arguable distinction between a style that is largely symptomatic of 'forced levity and grim desperation' and one in which such tones are part of a polemical spectrum that also includes examples of art's power to transcend circumstance, its capacity 'to free the intellect from the tyranny of the affects'. It is certainly possible to see both 'Envoi (1919)' and 'Medallion' as lyrics diversely maintaining that belief, if not that capacity; each modified by, and modifying, the clamour of the 'affects' within the sequence; the various voices of 'demand', 'censure', hysteria, exaggeration, mendacity, with which it reverberates.

The 'function of an art', so expressed, is an invocation not an Archimedean 'proof'; it is essentially one's feeling that things are so (an emphasis somewhat different from, and more vulnerable than, Hardy's poignant 'Hoping it might be so' yet pitched against not dissimilar 'affects' of common sense). It is a state of mind which Pound, in 1912, had the ingenuousness to admit: 'This difference, this dignity . . . must be conveyed . . . by the art of the verse structure, by something which exalts the reader, making him feel that he is in contact with something arranged more finely than the commonplace.' That reiterated 'something', which does not strike one as deliberate, or much deliberated, concedes the intense subjectivism with which objectivity may be proclaimed, and naïvely approximates to the resonances of 'Envoi (1919)' rather than to the nuances of 'Medallion'.

James's significance for Pound, in the early years, is registered in the emphasis which the younger man placed on the capacity for intense feeling matched by a 'capacious intelligence' and the 'incessant labour of minute observation'. 'The passion of it, the continual passion of it in this man who, fools said, didn't "feel". I have never yet found a man of emotion against whom idiots didn't raise this cry.' This sentence stands as a characteristic gesture of Pound's conviction. The world's obtuseness, imperviousness, its active or passive hostility to valour and vision, is not only the object of his denunciation; it is also the necessary circumstance, the context in which and against which valour and vision define themselves: 'In the gloom, the gold gathers the light against it.' If it were not for the darkness and the enemies' torches the beauty of factive *virtù* would not shine out so in defiance of that circumstance which the 'gathering' has in part transformed. The difference between 'Feeling of utter hopelessness in struggle for values', in Pound's comment on Upward's suicide, and 'In the gloom, the gold gathers the light against it', from Canto 11, the last of the 'Malatesta' Cantos, is all in the definition; the raw material is the same: the detritus of the Dantean *Malebolge* which Pound had begun to sift and assay in his first prose book *The Spirit of Romance*, compounded with 'the ανάγκη of modernity, cash necessity', 'the aimless turmoil and restlessness of humanity' in general; in particular, 'the violent against art, and the usurers', 'the devil-driven pandars', 'the still malignity of the traitor's wallow'. Malatesta, 'famous condottiere, military engineer, and patron of the arts', one of the great factive heroes of the *Cantos*, defines himself by resistant achievement: '. . . against the power that was . . . Sigismundo cut his notch'; *'templum aedificavit'*. The suicide of an 'old combattant' such as Allen Upward seemed a hopeless surrender of self-defining, self-vindicating *virtù*. 'The suicide is not serious from conviction', Pound wrote, years later in Canto 93, but 'from sheer physical depression'.

If you affirm that 'the function of an art is to free the intellect from the tyranny of the affects' the statement none the less remains embedded in affects; requires, indeed, those dispositions or predispositions to effect its freedom from them. Exacerbation and enhancement are to some extent correlative. In 'Envoi (1919)' the concept of 'time' is, as it remains for Pound, also a complex emotion simply stated. It is the inescapable natural attrition lamented by the Roman and Renaissance love-poets whom he greatly admired: Propertius ('nox tibi longa venit nec reditura dies') and Campion imitating Propertius ('When thou must home to shades of vnder ground') and Waller in that song

which acts as Pound's point of departure and remonstrance
('The common fate of all things rare'); it is also the domain of the
temporal, of 'the lords of the temporal world'. One of the
several inter-involved ways in which 'Time is the evil' is that it is
the continuum in which the lords of the temporal world
manifest their cruelty and their contempt. Pound is not such a
fool as to suppose that the continuum is describable only in
negative terms. Malatesta was a lord of the temporal world and
'Rhythm is a form cut into TIME.' But Pound, at times, grounds
himself on treacherous axioms as though they were indeed
truths of first inscription. The stubbornness of one's dogmatism,
the force of one's own hubris, are themselves factors in the
world's general arbitrariness, 'coercions', 'personal tyranny';
and 'anyone can run to excesses . . . It is hard to stand firm in the
middle.' It is worth recalling that Pound had begun to read
Confucius and Mencius, in French translations, as early as 1913,
under the guidance of Allen Upward ('Law of MOU is law of the
just middle, the pivot'; 'Kung employed the right word neither
in excess nor less than his meaning . . .').

It is one thing to maintain the principle of the 'just middle' and
the *mot juste*; it is another to find, in the articulation of one's 'lifelong, unchangeable passion', all the crucial terms pre-empted
by the very powers one most deplores: the 'prominent or
protuberant public figures', the ' "gargoyles" . . . poets, that is,
with high reputation, most of whose work has gone since into
the discard', by that 'Provincialism' which is 'ignorance plus a
lust after uniformity'. Instead of the 'just middle' one has 'a soft
terminology . . . an endless series of indefinite middles', 'the
pimps' paradise of indefinite verbiage'. In theory and principle
Pound was always entirely clear about the necessary counter-
measures. From at least the time of *The Spirit of Romance*, in
1910, and probably before, he had no doubt that the study and
imitation of Provençal and Tuscan poetry and poetic theory was
the focal point of a truly resistant and reformative virtuous craft.
His simultaneous and subsequent discoveries—Kung, Flaubert,
Gautier, the art of Arnold Dolmetsch in reviving seventeenth-
century instrumental music and song—did not contradict or
override the Provençal–Tuscan *paideuma* but arranged themselves

in correlative order around that focus. Arnaut Daniel, Guido Cavalcanti: in these men 'the preciseness of the description denotes . . . a clarity of imaginative vision'; 'it is in the spirit of this period to be precise'. Pound was clearly moved, and considered himself instructed (as who would not?), by the luminous implications of those lines in the thirty-third canto of the *Paradiso* in which 'substance and accidents and their customs' are bound together by love 'in such wise that that which I speak is a simple light'. It seems to have been Pound's lifelong endeavour to find the means whereby that Dantean conception could be registered in the demonstrable technicalities of English verse. It was, one may add, the intuition that, at the highest level of technical accomplishment, the 'simple' embraces and is embraced by 'substance and accidents' that, in the first and second decades of this century, suggested to Pound an alternative to the arrogant provincialism of American opinion on literary matters, its assumption that, as he sardonically reported, 'The style of 1870 is the final and divine revelation.' At the same time Provençal and Tuscan clarity of intelligence is equally a rebuke to the 'new, nickel-plated, triumphant' social mechanisms in America and Europe (epitomized in *Hugh Selwyn Mauberley* by 'pianola', 'kinema', 'steam yacht') which were rapidly ousting the 'courteous, tawdry, quiet old'. 'The traditional methods are not antiquated, nor are poets necessarily the atavisms which they seem', he declared in 1912. They are not antiquated, not atavisms, if one has in mind Dante's idea that you can bind the complex into a simple light or assents to the sensuous intellect of Cavalcanti's 'Donna mi prega'. None the less the statement pre-supposes that 'the traditional methods are not antiquated' will be understood in precisely those terms that the proposer had in mind and will not be welcomed as a piece of sympathetic Luddism by upholders of the 'courteous, tawdry, quiet old'. When Pound writes 'traditional methods' he does not mean 'derivative convention'. In 1912, no less than at the present day, this was a distinction not easily impressed upon the consensus.

When, in the first line of 'Envoi (1919)', the poet addresses his 'dumb-born book' he is echoing 'still-born' from the sixth poem of the sequence, an allusion to the unacclaimed achievement of

Chapter Five

Edward FitzGerald, author of *The Rubáiyát of Omar Khayyám*, a work which Pound admired, one of those master-craftsmen born out of their due time, a genus with which Pound to some extent aligned himself: 'The English Rubaiyat was still-born | In those days.' But 'dumb-born' is not 'still-born' after all. Pound's 'book', the twelve poems of the sequence which precede 'Envoi (1919)', is 'dumb-born' because the tradition of '*motz el son*', the art of perfectly matching words and melody, mastered by the Provençal poet-singers and practised for the last time in England by Campion and Lawes, has in its passing left lyric speech bereft of its truest *melopoeia*. Men like Gautier and Laforgue and Landor have reintroduced other virtues, 'hardness' and '*logopoeia*', and much may be done with these, as *Homage to Sextus Propertius* and the twelve poems of *Hugh Selwyn Mauberley* (Part I) manifestly demonstrate; even so 'Envoi (1919)' recognizes in its opening phrase that the music of its own unfolding will be the only *melopoeia* the 'book' will have. The book may be 'dumb-born' in the further sense that its audience must be assumed to be deaf to its language: its *logopoeia* as much as its *melopoeia*. In 1919, criticizing some poems sent to him by Natalie Barney, Pound observed 'you use words that are not archaic but simply dead.—The archaism has its use but the dead word can only serve in Laforguian irony.' The average poetry-reader of the *lustrum* 1915–20, secure enough in his ignorance of, or contempt for, Laforguian ironies, would be much less secure with the distinction that Pound was drawing between 'archaic' and 'dead'. At such periods, much of the attrition experienced by a writer in Pound's situation comes from the general muzziness of things, the immense labour of picking one's way, as he said, between the 'not quite it' and the 'not quite not it'. Incompatibility is not some peculiar act of bad faith; it is in the nature of circumstance itself; and that vulnerable archaic 'beauty', to the ardent and arduous defence of which Pound committed all his energies, would not, at first encounter, in any way disturb his esteemed great aunt under whose tutelage he had first visited Europe at the age of twelve and for whom 'the one adjective, beautiful . . .' sufficed, albeit 'with apologies', for everything European 'from Alps to San Marco and Titians . . . and to the glass filagrees of Murano'. And 'that song of Lawes', if we take it as token of the high achievement of seventeenth-century English song, would have been entirely sympathetic to the ears of those minor American lyrists of the late nineteenth and early twentieth centuries represented in the influential anthologies of Jessie B. Rittenhouse.

The first issues of Harriet Monroe's magazine *Poetry*, founded in 1912, do not appear wholly unlike Rittenhouse's *The Little Book of Modern Verse* which appeared in the following year. Ridgely Torrence and Madison Cawein, whose poem 'Waste Land' was included in the fourth issue, had been featured in Rittenhouse's *The Younger American Poets* of 1904, which also gave attention to the work of Louise Imogen Guiney, now best remembered for her devoted research into the life of Henry Vaughan, Mary McNeil Fenollosa who, some years later, entrusted Pound with the editing of her late husband's papers on the Chinese Written Character and the Japanese Noh, Lizette Woodworth Reese, author of *A Handful of Lavender*, and Arthur Upson, whose posthumous *Collected Poems* of 1909 included 'After a Dolmetsch Concert' and 'A Viola D'Amore, XVIth Century', dedicated 'to Arnold Dolmetsch'. The first of these poems by Upson was reprinted in *The Little Book of Modern Verse*. Pound met Dolmetsch in 1913 and published tributes to his work in 1915 and 1917. Dolmetsch became for Pound one of several mentors in the different arts who showed that, rightly understood, the 'archaic' disciplines were the key to 'mak[ing] it new'. Pound also concluded that the massive ignorance concerning the old music which Dolmetsch was endeavouring to make known, music that had 'once been the pleasure of the many', amounted to 'a judgment on democracy'. For Pound the old music starts with 'the vortex of pattern' and is radically distinct from 'impressionist or "emotional" music'. 'This old music was not theatrical. You played it yourself as you read a book of precision . . . It was not an interruption but a concentration.' The significance, such as it is, of Upson's 'After a Dolmetsch Concert' is that it is 'impressionist or "emotional" ', a theatrical interruption of concentration on precise and more enduring patterns ('Out of the conquered Past | Unravishable

Beauty; | Hearts that are dew and dust | Rebuking the dream of Death'). To the ignorant ear, conscious of theme but not of timbre or nuance, Upson and Pound would be speaking the same language, since they were discoursing upon the same subject and since the difference between Upson's derivative Keatsian 'Unravishable Beauty' and Pound's new-made Waller ('Go, dumb-born book | Tell her that sang me once that song of Lawes') is precisely the kind of distinction that the '*lustrum*' could not attune to. As Miss Rittenhouse wrote of Lizette Woodworth Reese, her work showed 'constant affinity with Herrick, though it is rarely so blithe' or again 'She would recapture the blitheness of Herrick, the valor of Lovelace.' Lovelace's 'To Althea, from Prison' merits an allusion in *The Pisan Cantos* ('at my grates no Althea') but 'lavender', a word cultivated by Miss Reese, was for Pound a term of denigration, as in the 'olde lavender' of the 'perfumed writers' or in 'the "sweet dim faded lavender" tone' of James at his most etiolated. As we have observed, the opposition is clear enough in principle, persuading one that the necessary distinctions can be communicated in practice. In practice, however, the matter appears more complex and more elusive. In 1938 Pound would be praising Chaucer's sense of inherited song modes 'worn smooth in the mind, so that the words take the quality for singing'. The crux here is 'worn smooth'. It is one thing to treat of smoothness as a factive adjunct within the tradition of '*motz el son*'; it is another to encounter the anodyne smoothness, 'the "sweet dim faded lavender" tone', of the effete neo-cavaliers. Pound's problem in 'Envoi (1919)' is that, in seeking to restore the quality of *melopoeia* as he understood it to be inherent in the craft of seventeenth-century English song, he comes perilously close to being thought to endorse the 'blitheness', etc. that Miss Rittenhouse associated with the cavalier lyric. It is an extreme form of the problem that all poets face: in making a choice one is also drawing down, as though by natural gravity, that which one has not chosen but which is an inextricable part of the 'circumstance'. Pound said 'you cannot call a man an artist until he shows himself capable of reticence and of restraint, until he shows himself in some degree master of the forces which beat upon him'. It *is* a question of 'degree': 'if 'Envoi' behaves cavalierly towards reticence, 'Medallion' modifies what we think of the value of 'restraint'. This caveat makes all the more urgent and poignant those claims to absolute judgement which Pound from time to time puts forward on behalf of poets and poetry. In these congeries, however, Miss Rittenhouse, for all her masterful brokerage of the extrinsic and ephemeral, is finally shown to be a tiro in matters of intrinsic value.

Pound, from his juvenilia through to *The Pisan Cantos* and *Drafts and Fragments* . . ., steadily emphasized the qualities of affirmation, love, praise, veneration: 'By what characteristic may we know the divine forms? | By beauty.' In his imaginary conversation with Rabelais, 'An Anachronism at Chinon', first published in 1917, he has the modern 'student' observe that the spirit of the Renaissance humanist's classroom is now found only 'among a few scattered enthusiasts, men half ignorant in the present "scholarly" sense, but alive with the spirit of learning, avid of truth, avid of beauty, avid of strange and out of the way bits of knowledge'. The dangerously rhetorical 'avid of . . .' thrice repeated, the seemingly unguarded 'beauty', are protected, though only in part, by the irony of the title, 'An Anachronism . . .'. In his autobiographical fragment *Indiscretions* (1920) Pound remarked that his father was 'the naivest man who ever possessed sound sense' and throughout his own work, from the early *The Spirit of Romance* and *Patria Mia* to the last fragments, he remains convinced that one ought to be able to proclaim the virtues and values simply, directly, even 'naïvely', if that is how it is fated to appear in the world's eyes: 'Till change hath broken down | All things save Beauty alone'; 'What thou lov'st well shall not be reft from thee'. At the same time he is, in his critical writings, breaking down the simple coherence of 'Beauty' as it stands proclaimed in 'Envoi (1919)' into a number of facets: 'Beauty is a brief gasp between one cliché and another'; 'Beauty *is* an accusation'; or (in *The Pisan Cantos*) ' "beauty is difficult" sd | Mr Beardsley'. The matter is further perplexed by Pound's awareness of 'conflicts in himself between modernism and passéism', his need to move away from the 'archaizing Wardour Street of his first collections'. In a letter to James Joyce, in July 1917, he referred to the 'mellifluous archaism' of a version from Horace on which he was currently engaged. In his first prose book *The Spirit of Romance* one encounters such belletrisms as 'sheer poetic magic', 'infinitely more beautiful', 'the noblest love lyric in the world', 'nothing more or less than the magical quality of poetry'; and in the later tributes to the music-making of the Dolmetsch family his evocation of the old music ('tones clear as brown amber') is precious rather than precise. With such phrases it is not easy to determine whether we are picking up a few pieces of parochial detritus or whether Pound, grimly aware that he is proselytizing in the enemy's country, is pragmatically trading a few catch-words in the 'provincial' tongue as the necessary price for being given any sort of hearing, even the most cursory and indifferent. Parallel with this runs a zealous attempt at definition, begun early and persisted in for many years, in which 'the beautiful' is equated with 'τὸ καλόν'. It is likely that Pound first encountered the concept when reading Coleridge in 1907: the proposal that the Greek words for 'the beautiful' embody the sense of like calling to like, a sense reflected in the (false) etymology. When, in the third lyric of *Hugh Selwyn Mauberley*, he writes 'We see τὸ καλόν | Decreed in the market place' the irony scarcely needs glossing, though one recollects a letter of William James recording 'To Kalon' in 1900 as the label on an American claret.

The kind of ironic enjambment in 'τὸ καλόν | Decreed in the market place', the conflation, in the last line of the same poem, of the Olympian victory-wreath with the tin *cache-sexe* for nude statues cited in the brusque note to his nervous publisher Elkin Mathews, is a style designed to mime and master a particular ambience. He describes such circumstances, in his obituary on A. R. Orage, as the 'quicksand of obfuscation, the ignorance, the non-correlation, the irritation of the jostled, the gross silence of hired concealers . . .'. One of the discoveries of 'modernist' poetry has been the technique of transposing the hopeless 'irritation of the jostled', 'the gross silence of hired concealers', into the kind of rapid juxtapositions and violent lacunae that one finds in the third and fourth poems of *Hugh Selwyn Mauberley*— phrase callously jostling with phrase, implication merging into implication ('pli selon pli'), sententiae curtly abandoned. These become key instruments of the 'intelligence at bay'. This too is a phrase of Pound's. It occurs in a memorial tribute of 1915 to Rémy de Gourmont celebrating, among other virtues, his beneficent influence on writers younger than himself, 'a vortex of twenty men, and among them five or six of the most intelligent young men in Paris . . . These men were plotting a gigantic blague. A "blague" when it is a fine blague is a satire upon stupidity, an attack. It is the weapon of intelligence at bay; of intelligence fighting against an alignment of odds.' That 'blague' was a particular piece of tactics, a farcical mock election parodying a journalistic penchant for titling nonentities 'Prince des Penseurs', 'Prince des Poètes' or 'Prince des Conteurs'. By 1918 Pound was using the term of Henry James, calling him 'the great blagueur', referring, in the same essay, to his 'blague and benignity'. *Homage to Sextus Propertius*, that '*collage* of poker-faced misreadings', contains strong elements of blague; so does the third poem in the *Mauberley* sequence. But 'Envoi (1919)' seems, on first acquaintance, to hold itself aloof from such tactics:

> Tell her that sheds
> Such treasure in the air,
> Recking naught else but that her graces give
> Life to the moment,
> I would bid them live
> As roses might, in magic amber laid,
> Red overwrought with orange and all made
> One substance and one colour
> Braving time.

What is 'braving time'? It is to challenge, to defy, with a tincture of 'bravura', the 'display of daring or defiance; brilliancy of execution', as in 'a passage or piece of music requiring great skill and spirit in its execution, written to task the artist's powers'. 'Envoi (1919)' is a bravura performance. In such lines Pound is, perhaps, seeking to answer one of his own earlier questions. In 1913, quoting some lines of Beddoes, he had asked 'Can a man write poetry in a purely archaic dialect?' and had answered

'Presumably he can, and Beddoes has done so'. In the year of this poem's composition he remarked to Natalie Barney 'The archaism has its use.' We should ask ourselves what 'use' the archaism may be thought to have in 'Envoi (1919)'. For one thing, it takes the various facets and possibilities of 'Beauty' as Pound tried to define it or as he had heard it defined ('Beauty *is* an accusation', ' "beauty is difficult" sd | Mr Beardsley') and concentrates them in something that, in 1912, he had called the 'beauty of the means'. 'Labour on the TECHNIQUE of singable words is honourable labour', he would write in 1938, adding 'God knows I worked in the dark from 1905 onwards, and the light has come very slowly.' Pound also reminded Binyon that, years previously, he had heard him say 'Slowness is beauty', which 'struck me as very odd in 1908 (when I certainly did not believe it) and has stayed with me ever since'. Those who have left accounts of Pound's manner of reading aloud his own and others' work have recorded the 'strongly marked time', the slow pace of his delivery: 'He reads it that slow. It's stately, majestical'; 'Rhythm extremely exact and tempo very slow'. It would seem that a number of things slowly came together, from the technical and ethical peripheries, all focused upon a sense of tempo and all understood as the necessary basis for accurate judgement and for any genuine act of swift intuition. Pound's theory of the 'great bass' in music is that 'down below the lowest note synthesized by the ear and "heard" there are slower vibrations . . . The whole question of tempo, and of a main base in all musical structure resides in use of these frequencies.'

Such words as 'tempo', 'structure', and 'frequencies' brought here into arbitrary collocation with reminiscences of the slow pace of his delivery may suggest a claim on my part that 'Envoi (1919)' converts the idea 'Slowness is beauty' into a pattern of metrics that can be mathematically demonstrated. I make no such claim. Pound reads 'that slow' because it feels right; and it feels right because 'slow pace' is an ethos before it is anything else. In his reading of *The Divine Comedy* Pound's eye and ear were attracted by those episodes in the *Inferno* and the *Purgatorio* describing Dante's encounters with Sordello and other worthy albeit flawed and troubled spirits 'delli occhi onesta e tarda', 'con occhi tardi e gravi'. He emphatically associated these phrases with Henry James, 'The massive head, the slow uplift of the hand, *gli occhi onesti e tardi* . . . the lightning incision'. It is to be observed that 'slowness' is the necessary ethical and physical preparative for that 'quality of a sudden vision of intuition or glimpse into things', that 'inevitable swiftness and rightness in a given field' which, for Pound, was the essential *virtù* of 'genius'. Here too he is in accord with Allen Upward, who noted in his autobiography 'I wrote *The New Word* in a fortnight. I had been composing it for twenty-five years.'

The factive 'swiftness', whatever might be supposed to the contrary, has nothing in common with the rapidity of access and communication found desirable by contemporary civilization: the 'kinetic' ('prose kinema'). In February 1916, in an essay on 'Mr James Joyce and the Modern Stage', Pound wrote 'Professionals tell us: "Oh, they have quickened the tempo. Ibsen is too slow," and the like. So we have Shaw; that is to say, Ibsen with the sombre reality taken out . . .'. Slowness seems to be concomitant, therefore, with a certain kind of integrity of the imagination, 'full of certitude and implacable, and unswerving', the kind that tends to be rejected by the 'compleasant', the accommodating, as 'naïve' or 'reactionary' or 'archaic' or slow on the uptake and that finds itself punished in some way, 'at bay', set about by malice and misunderstanding, branded by its own purgatorial suffering, and yet imbued perhaps with a 'sombre reality', perhaps with 'something which exalts the reader, making him feel that he is in contact with something arranged more finely than the commonplace'. One would claim no more for Pound's performance of his own work, as on the 1939 disc which includes a reading of 'Envoi (1919)', than that it sounds 'full of certitude and implacable, and unswerving' and might 'exalt' the listener, making him feel that he is in contact with something arranged more finely than the commonplace. The pace and pitch of the voice do not solve the 'whole question of tempo' as it affects one's understanding of this and other poems; but they emphatically confirm an attitude of mind and must, of course, be susceptible to the charge of vocal attitudinizing and moral portentousness. If, however, one were asked, on such

97

grounds, to concede that 'Envoi (1919)' reads as 'impression-istically' as Arthur Upson's 'After a Dolmetsch Concert' the concession should not be made. It confuses the accidental with the intrinsic. When Upson writes 'Hearts that are dew and dust | Rebuking the dream of Death' the statement is otiose, the verb collapses into its own vacuity. When Pound recites what he has written—'One substance and one colour | Braving time'—his word 'braving' is already so placed, so cunningly circumstanced, that it can sustain not only the intermingled, interacting portentousness and irony of the poem itself but also the overweening, gratuitous sonorities of Pound's recital.

'Envoi (1919)' is required to carry a weightier and more complex syntax than is Waller's 'Goe lovely Rose', upon which it is based. The laboured conditionals ('Hadst thou but . . .', 'Then were there . . .', 'I would . . .', 'As roses might . . .', 'May be as fair . . .', 'Might, in new ages . . .') admit the power of the 'accidentals and imperfections'. At the same time the verse insists on the melopoeic quality of rhythm and cadence, as though this were indivisible from 'a certain verity of feeling'. In an essay on the sculptor Brancusi, published some two years after *Mauberley*, Pound suggested that 'perhaps every artist at one time or another believes in a sort of elixir or philosopher's stone produced by the sheer perfection of his art; by the alchemical sublimation of the medium; the elimination of accidentals and imperfections'. 'Sheer perfection' is one of those usages, like Mr Asquith's 'almost indefinable, never mistakable' essence of 'style', which, while saluting a lyric sublimation, succeed only in perpetuating a sense of poetical redundancy. The concluding words of 'Envoi (1919)', 'Till change hath broken down | All things save Beauty alone', maintain the idea of 'sheer perfection' though at some remove from the complacent aplomb with which that phrase is commonly uttered. Beauty, which for Pound included the 'consummation of métier', a crafted entity, the 'melody which most in-centres the soul', or an ' "absolute rhythm", a rhythm . . . which corresponds exactly to the emotion or shade of emotion to be expressed', is, in the drift and occasion and contexture of things, hardly to be wrested from the subjective impressions of Herbert Asquith or Jessie B.

Rittenhouse promulgated as matters of public acceptance and judgement.

Miss Rittenhouse had met Pound in New York early in 1911 'on his one and only visit' to the Poetry Society of America. Seven years later, in the January 1918 issue of *The Bookman*, she reviewed the American edition of *Lustra . . . with Earlier Poems*. Though she found 'much beauty' in 'the Chinese section, *Cathay*' and welcomed the reappearance, among the earlier poems, of the 1912 collection *Ripostes*, particularly its 'haunting and lovely poem' 'Δώρια', her review as a whole was unfavourable, expressing strong disapproval of Pound's 'bewildering medley of tongues and styles' and asking 'What is his own voice, his own style, his own individuality?' Though she conceded that, out of this 'poetic scrap-bag' of languages and cultures, Pound 'weaves for himself a fabric of song which might be beautiful had [he] the art to make it so' the qualification was tendentious. In praising Pound's earlier work she had already acknowledged his artistry. Her present objection was rather to the moral flaw, as she conceived it, in his recent intentions. Demanding 'something worthy of the inspiration' and finding that Pound had 'repudiated his earlier manner', the style which she had been pleased to approve, Miss Rittenhouse accused him of setting 'a trap for his critics'.

The meaning and implications of 'something of beauty and value', 'something worthy of the inspiration', and suchlike phrases must be teased out from among the lyric congeries of Lizette Woodworth Reese, Arthur Upson, Madison Cawein, Clinton Scollard, Orrick Johns, and others, who gave 'charm and romance to the immediate thing'. While not claiming that 'Go, dumb-born book' stands as a direct riposte to the prejudicate opinions of the *Bookman* review, one may fairly regard it as a poem 'at bay', confronting not only the fragile appeal but also the heavy proscriptions of the Rittenhouse ethos.

It is as much the strength as the weakness of 'Envoi (1919)' that its melopoeic certitude does not annul the numerous uncertainties. If we set this poem alongside 'The Return', composed some seven years earlier ('See, they return; ah, see the tentative | Movements, and the slow feet, | The trouble in the pace and the uncertain | Wavering!'), where the rhythm is 'reflective', composed 'to the feel of the thing', or if one thinks of 'The Coming of War: Actaeon', which had appeared in *Lustra*, the later poem seems in some respects retrograde. Pound was to say, reflecting upon the early period many years later, in *The Pisan Cantos*, 'To break the pentameter, that was the first heave'; and this is indeed what 'The Return' and 'The Coming of War: Actaeon' succeed in doing. But in the second stanza of 'Envoi (1919)' the nine irregular lines are six regular pentameters in disguise. The 'detail of surface' is not quite 'in accord with the root in justice'. One may surmise, therefore, that Pound has his attention focused on something other than that '[bringing] forth from the inner nature' to which his concept of 'absolute rhythm' was devoted. 'Rhythm' here is not easily separated from metrical subterfuge; it is not absolute but relative, reminiscent, an adjunct to something else; and that something else is not entirely divorced from 'blague'. But whereas blague, as Pound seems to envisage it, begins with pomp and ends in derision, this poem emerges from circumstances of derision ('Wrong from the start', 'Bent resolutely on wringing lilies from the acorn') into its defiant, self-conscious *melopoeia*: 'poetry which moves by its music, whether it be a music in the words or an aptitude for, or suggestion of, accompanying music.'

This 'self-consciousness' is a crux which I have, perhaps contentiously, introduced. Though one is not obliged to think of it as a Prufrockian nervous inhibition, it undeniably implies a sharp apprehension, a shade more vulnerable than self-awareness, of the circumstances in which the self speaks and acts. The actual, historical protagonist of *Homage to Sextus Propertius* had been, in Pound's estimation, both keenly aware and intensely self-conscious, Laforgue's precursor in the discovery and practice of 'good verbalism', the deployment of 'the word in some special relation to "usage" '. *Homage* itself is an exercise in this mode, as are the first and third poems of the *Mauberley* sequence. 'E. P. Ode pour l'Election de son Sepulchre' is cast as a deriding of E.P. by the triumphalism of current 'usage', the rhetoric of the political and literary *imperium*. Yet even as he was preparing his logopoeic *Homage* for publication Pound suggested that, in certain cases, logopoeia may be 'the utterance of clever people in despair'. Work on *Homage* and *Mauberley* proceeded concurrently with the composition of the earliest *Cantos*. Versions of the first three were printed at the end of the first American edition of *Lustra*, where Miss Rittenhouse found them incoherent but preferable to 'Contemporiana'. In December 1919 Pound wrote to his father that he had 'done cantos 5, 6, 7, each is more incomprehensible than the one preceding it; I don't know what's to be done about it'. 'Incomprehensible', used like this, makes a mockery of despair; it is a word at bay.

'Envoi (1919)', defying the incomprehensible and the despairing in its 'canorous lyric measures', yet embarrassingly placed in relation, or disrelation, to the sequence as a whole, stands for 'what's to be done about it' and for what cannot be 'done' about it: 'it' in this case being fairly typified (I would argue) by the kind of canorous lyric measures that Miss Rittenhouse preferred to the measures of *Lustra* or by Prime Minister Asquith's 1919 tribute to 'the sovereign quality of Style'. Pound's melopoeia is itself drawn into 'a dance of the intelligence among words and ideas and modification of ideas and characters' since what is 'modified' in 'Envoi (1919)' is by implication the question 'What is his own voice, his own style, his own individuality?' The absolute is brought back to become a part of the relative and the conditional, the not quite it and the not quite not it; but, so circumstanced, is all the more fully and directly affirmed. Lyric utterance stands as witness to a faith in 'sheer perfection' even while it is standing scrutiny as a piece of evidence in the natural history of such belief. ' "[B]eauty is difficult" sd | Mr Beardsley.' When Pound put that phrase into *The Pisan Cantos*, his source, one supposes, was Yeats, the sixteenth chapter of 'The Tragic Generation': 'I said to [Beardsley] once, "You have never done anything to equal your Salome with the head of John the Baptist." I think that for the moment he was sincere when he replied, "Yes, yes; but beauty is so difficult." ' Yeats was in two minds about Beardsley; divided between admiration for his 'noble courage' and despair at the 'spirit of mockery' which he saw as more and more withering in its effect. 'Yes, yes; but beauty is so difficult' is therefore to be taken both as an act of witness, a testimony, and as an abdication of responsibility. 'For the moment', Yeats thinks, 'he was sincere'. The difference between the pitch of Yeats's concession, or caveat, and the cadence of 'Envoi (1919)' is marked by a proximity of phrase: 'Recking naught else but that her graces give | Life to the moment . . .'. As I see it, Pound sets himself the task, as much in this poem as in *The Pisan Cantos* some twenty-five years later, of transposing 'bravery' from the domain of the merely 'sincere' (which is ephemeral and solipsistic) into a form of 'substance' and 'colour' successfully detached from the ephemeral. The strength and weakness of 'Envoi (1919)' is that we are given a not wholly satisfactory process in the guise of a satisfyingly finished piece. Integrity is in the mood (largely the moods of the verb), otiosity is in the mode (those lyrical affirmatives scarcely to be distinguished from the school of Rittenhouse). Integrity, so circumstanced, relapses into the merely sincere; and beauty—against the grain of the argument—remains 'a brief gasp between one cliché and another'.

Notes to the Text

I   Unhappy Circumstances

1   *Aubrey records . . . worke.' Aubrey's 'Brief Lives'*, ed. A. Clark, 2 vols. (Oxford, 1898), i. 340–1.

When Hobbes . . . the rest'. Leviathan, ed. C. B. Macpherson (Harmondsworth, 1968), 209.

The Art of Complaisance . . . See George Etherege, *The Man of Mode*, ed. J. Barnard (London, 1979), xxxiii–xxxiv (editor's introduction); P. Hammond, *John Oldham and the Renewal of Classical Culture* (Cambridge, 1983), 205.

accommodated in the word 'compleasance' itself. See W. W. Skeat, *A Concise Etymological Dictionary of the English Language*, 2nd, revised, edn. (Oxford, 1885), 355: 'Please . . . L. *placere*, to please. Allied to *placare*, to appease.' Cf. ibid., s.vv. 'complacent', 'complaisant', 'placable'. It is the intimate relationship of power with appeasement, of pre-emption with flexibility and obligingness, that is the characteristic in numerous instances of English style: whether in Sir Robert Howard's genial subjective coerciveness on matters of taste or in the way in which Professors Bradbury and Bigsby take possession of 'our' and 'ours' ('Accordingly, this continuing series is an endeavour to look at some of the most important writers of our time'; 'Our wish is that, in their very variety of approach and emphasis, these books will stimulate interest in and understanding of the vitality of a living literature which, because it is contemporary, is especially ours'.—'General Editors' Preface' to the series 'Contemporary Writers' (London, 1982–   )). 'Especially ours' elides the indeterminate commonality of 'our time' with the elusive determination 'our wish'. It is 'our wish' to oblige the clichés of current conversation ('we live in a major creative time', 'the works of major post-war writers'); it is also 'our' wish to present such authors as Margaret Drabble and John Le Carré as 'most important writers'. '*Our*' time must here mean '*your* time made placable to *our* cultural scenario'. If they truly meant 'our time' they would have to take account of e.g. *my* time. Margaret Drabble and John Le Carré do not figure among the most important writers of my time, but my scepticism, and the views of those who might share my scepticism, are effectively excluded from consideration by being included in the complacent locution. This appeal to the supposed consensus seems to me in direct conflict with Dr Johnson's meaning when he wrote that Gray's 'Elegy' 'abounds with images which find a mirrour in every mind, and with sentiments to which every bosom returns an echo', though Bradbury and Bigsby doubtless 'rejoice to concur with the common reader' according to their understanding of that term. To the suggestion that Johnson's statement is itself merely a matter of opinion delivered with aplomb I would reply that his priorities strike me as being right and that he avoids blurring or eliding the implications of his words. For Johnson it is the *poem* that establishes and maintains the tone; the sensibility of the 'common reader' may be judged by his or her capacity to echo or reflect its intrinsic qualities. The fact that, in the case of Gray's 'Elegy', so many common readers have manifested this capability is a tribute to the poem itself rather than to 'the spirit of contemporary criticism'.

It was observed . . . obliging'. In the sermon preached at her funeral. See Aubrey, ed. cit. i. 119; and see Hammond, op. cit. 205.

2 *'patience . . . domination.* Barnard, op. cit. xxxiv.

Etherege's . . . change it.' The Man of Mode, ed. cit. 91.

In Hobbes's terms . . . Intractable'. Leviathan, ed. cit. 210.

'An Ode . . . aloofe'. Ben Jonson, ed. C. H. Herford and P. Simpson, 11 vols. (Oxford, 1925–52), viii. 174–5.

3 *Harriet's depiction . . . 'poignancy'.* Ed. cit. 142 and xxxviii (editor's introduction).

as Dr Johnson said . . . at ease. Johnson: Prose and Poetry, ed. M. Wilson (London, 1966), 811.

the author of the 'Epilogue' . . . Rochester. See C. E. Ward, The Life of John Dryden (Chapel Hill, 1961), 83, 109, 114.

by 1697 . . . John Dennis. See Ward, Life, 240, 250–1, on Dryden's 'refusal to compromise'; and see G. McFadden, Dryden the Public Writer 1660–1685 (Princeton, 1978), 91: 'As for Dryden, he chose to be loyal to James when he clearly perceived it to be ruinous'; 132: 'Mulgrave's . . . steady adherence to the cause of the Duke of York'. See also DNB articles. I am indebted to Ian Jack for an opinion.

4 *The matter . . . paronomasia.* See P. G. W. Glare (ed.), Oxford Latin Dictionary (Oxford, 1982), 1168: 'negōtium . . . [neg-(NEQVE) + OTIVM].'

that 'vacation . . . ease'. A Discourse of the Common Weal of this Realm of England (written c.1552), ed. E. Lamond (Cambridge, 1893), 10; Sir William Davenant's Gondibert, ed. D. F. Gladish (Oxford, 1971), 24.

Francis Meres . . . Horace. Elizabethan Critical Essays, ed. G. G. Smith, 2 vols. (Oxford, 1904), ii. 313.

Milton . . . men'). Milton: Complete Shorter Poems, ed. J. Carey (London, 1971), 151; Complete Prose Works of John Milton, 8 vols. (New Haven and London, 1953–), i. 804: 'Not such a lazy life is implied here as modern usage would suggest. Ease simply meant freedom from physical labor; leisure, freedom and opportunity for study' (editorial note by R. A. Haug). See also: 'So that being now quiet from State-Adversaries and publick Contests, he had leisure again for his own Studies and private Designs' (Edward Phillips, *The Life of Mr John Milton* (1694), in *The Early Lives of Milton*, ed. H. Darbishire (London, 1932), 72).

Dryden's letters . . . epilogues. E.g. *The Letters of John Dryden*, ed. C. E. Ward (Durham, NC, 1942), 13, 23, 113; *The Prologues and Epilogues of John Dryden: A Critical Edition* by W. B. Gardner (New York, 1951), 23, 32, 91, 102–3.

'by incoherent . . . neglect'. John Locke, *An Essay Concerning Human Understanding*, ed. P. M. Nidditch (Oxford, 1975), 7.

'The only . . . worry'. *Impact: Essays on Ignorance and the Decline of American Civilization* by Ezra Pound, ed. N. Stock (Chicago, 1960), 218. See also Ezra Pound, *Gaudier–Brzeska: A Memoir*, new edn. (Hessle, 1960), 64–5. Cf. *The Letters of Wyndham Lewis*, ed. W. K. Rose (London, 1963), 340–1. See also 'Whoever is not in the possession of leisure can hardly be said to possess independence. They talk of the *dignity of work.* Bosh. True Work is the *necessity* of poor humanity's earthly condition. The dignity is in leisure. Besides, 99 hundredths of all the *work* done in the world is either foolish and unnecessary, or harmful and wicked' (Herman Melville, in a letter of 5 Sept. 1877, cited in Jay Leyda, *The Melville Log: A Documentary Life of Herman Melville 1819–1891*, 2 vols. (New York, 1951) ii. 765).

Dryden and Pound . . . society of his day. And one may add G. McFadden's observation: 'Throughout his whole life [Dryden's] record clearly shows a pattern of generous encouragement to younger writers, beyond a parallel in our literature until Ezra Pound came along' (op. cit. 149).

5   *'platitude . . . aridity'.* *Selected Prose*, ed. W. Cookson (London, 1973), 361; *Literary Essays*, ed. T. S. Eliot (London, 1954), 70.

'you cannot . . . him'. *Patria Mia* (Chicago, 1950), 47.

His 'choice . . . his 'technic' . . . E.g. 'Postscript to the Reader [of *Virgil's Aeneis*]', in *The Poems of John Dryden*, ed. J. Kinsley, 4 vols. (Oxford, 1958), 1424; *Literary Essays of Ezra Pound*, ed. cit., 115; *Ah, Sweet Dancer: W. B. Yeats/Margot Ruddock*, ed. R. McHugh (London, 1970), 81.

Hobbes's definition . . . thing'. Leviathan, ed. cit., 151, 295. See the excellent discussion in C. B. Macpherson, *The Political Theory of Possessive Individualism: Hobbes to Locke* (Oxford, 1962), 219–20.

6 *The state . . . hands'*. J. Clapham, *The Bank of England: A History*, 2 vols. (Cambridge, 1944), i. 26, 35–6; W. M. Acres, *The Bank of England from Within*, 2 vols. (London, 1931), i. 66; Dryden, *Letters*, ed. cit. 170, n. 4.

the virtues of 'labor . . . richness. Virgil, *The Eclogues and Georgics*, ed. R. D. Williams (Basingstoke, 1979), 144 n. 199; 136–7 nn. 43–70; 139–40 nn. 118–46.

'improbus'. See Williams, ed. cit. 141. nn. 145–6.

7 *'quid meruere . . . labores?'* Ovid, *Metamorphoses*, with an English translation by F. J. Miller, 2 vols. (London and New York, 1916), ii. 372.

the word 'silly'. The Oxford English Dictionary, 2nd edn., 20 vols. (Oxford, 1989), xv. 478; xiv. 879.

Those are Davenant's phrases. In *Gondibert*, ed. cit. 24.

'hominumque . . . labores' Williams, ed. cit. 32; 140 nn. 118–21: 'the hard toil of men and oxen alike.'

'durum genus'. Ibid. 30; 137 n. 63: 'an aetiological explanation of why men are hardy.' I am indebted to Katy Ricks for her advice.

8 *'hiems curasque resolvit'* Ibid. 36. I owe the point about Dryden's reworking of these lines to David Ricks.

'aut oculis . . . talpae. Ibid. 33; 143 nn. 181–3.

Mildmay Fane . . . negotium. Otia Sacra (1648) by Mildmay Fane, Second Earl of Westmorland, Facsimile, ed. D. M. Friedman (Delmar, NY, 1975), viii (editor's introduction). 'Competitive *negotium*' is Friedman's phrase, as is 'virtues of contemplative quiet'.

9 *'Rimes' . . . times'* Ed. cit. 174.

('Bidding me . . . surfet'). Ed. cit. 8, 15, 25, 26, 33, 34. There is a proper use for pleonasm, as Milton demonstrates in Satan's speeches in *Paradise Regain'd*. This effective 'mannerism' has been well documented and appraised by John Carey in *John Milton: Complete Shorter Poems*, paperback edn. (London, 1971), 426–7.

'a very just . . . display'. Ed. cit. 811.

'Few things . . . do.' Letter to the Reverend Dr Wetherell . . ., 12 Mar. 1776. *Boswell's Life of Johnson*, ed. G. B. Hill, rev. edn., 6 vols. (Oxford, 1934), ii. 424.

'frigid tranquillity' . . . empty sounds'. Prose and Poetry, 323.

'just as a man's language . . . limitation'. L. Binyon, *The Flight of the Dragon* (London, 1911), 14, quoted in Pound, *Pavannes and Divagations* (Norfolk, Conn., 1958), 149. Pound's rendering differs very slightly from the source. I have retained Binyon's wording.

10 *the 'subjective element'.* Binyon, op. cit. 14.

'*. . . the "statesman . . . idiom'.* ABC of Reading* (London, 1951), 34.

his indignation . . . cloth. Prose and Poetry, 943.

'Business' has always been . . . fulfilment. E.g. 'since that little fancy and liberty I once enjoy'd, is now fetter'd in business of more unpleasant Natures' (Sir Robert Howard, *The Great Favourite, Or, The Duke of Lerma* (London, 1668), Facsimile edn. (New York, 1975), A2ᵛ; 'the Multiplicity, the Cares, and the Vexations of your Imployment, have betray'd you from your self, and given you up into the Possession of the Publick. You are Robb'd of your Privacy and Friends, and scarce any hour of your Life you can call your own' (Dryden, 'The Epistle Dedicatory' to *All for Love* (13: 8). One may compare and contrast 'I often had occasion to remark, Johnson loved business, loved to have his wisdom actually operate on real life' (James Boswell, 20 Mar. 1776, ed. cit. ii. 441; cf. iv. 86–7). 'I have been to hear the Lord Chief Justice sum up [in the Tichborne case] . . . It is interesting to see that there is no other way, in the long run at least, for carrying on important things than the way of carrying on the unimportant ones. Business must be businesslike. The day of judgment however will be dramatic throughout' (G. M. Hopkins, *Further Letters . . .*, ed. C. C. Abbott, 2nd edn. revised and enlarged (London, 1956), 60, 24 Feb. 1874). Professor Sir Walter Raleigh wittily observed 'I lead the life of a defaulting debtor . . . chivied by people who behave as if they had lent me money' (*The Letters of Sir Walter Raleigh: 1879–1922*, ed. Lady Raleigh, 2 vols. (London, 1926), i, p. xviii). How far is it true that to have one's 'wisdom actually operate on real life' is at the same time to 'betray . . . you from your self'? To what extent is there validity in the suggestion that to be thus betrayed 'from your self' is a necessary 'real life' corrective to a Romantic absolutist aesthetic (e.g. *The Letters of Ezra Pound: 1907–1941*, ed. D. D. Paige (London, 1951), 249)? 'When will you be giving us another volume of your verses, Mr X?' Is the particular relish of the word 'give' its being at once a 'little fancy' and a demand-note? Mr X might justly bridle at being so chivvied by brisk assumptions about *otium*. Judged by Johnson's and Hopkins's standards, however, his understandable resentment and self-pity could appear merely otiose. It is further to be remarked that Crashaw's anonymous panegyrist precludes our dithering on either side of the question: 'hee made his skill in Poetry, Musicke, Drawing, Limming, graving . . . to

bee but his subservient recreations for vacant houres, not the grand businesse of his soule ('The Preface to the Reader', *Steps to the Temple* (1646), in *The Poems of Richard Crashaw* ed. L. C. Martin (Oxford, 1927), 76). This too may be taken as a necessary corrective to some of the other arguments cited here (including, of course, my own).

'desidiosa . . . negotium'. I am indebted to M. T. Griffin, *Seneca: A Philosopher in Politics* (Oxford, 1976), especially pp. 315–66, 'The Philosopher on Political Participation'. The two phrases which I quote appear on p. 318. The Senecan oxymoron can still be heard, in the last decade of the eighteenth century, in Arthur Murphy's 'translation, or rather imitation' of Johnson's Latin poem composed 'after revising and enlarging the English . . . Dictionary': 'He curs'd the industry, inertly strong, | In creeping toil that could persist so long . . .' See *An Essay on the Life and Genius of Samuel Johnson LL.D.* by Arthur Murphy Esq. (London, 1792), 82–5.

11 *'Although the Management . . . way.'* Samuel Butler, *Prose Observations*, ed. H. de Quehen (Oxford, 1979), 194.

the *'Amphion'* . . . *Spaniards. The Poems and Letters of Andrew Marvell*, ed. H. M. Margoliouth, 3rd edn., rev. P. Legouis and E. E. Duncan-Jones, 2 vols. (Oxford, 1971), i. 109, 123.

'Resistless genious'. Marvell, ed. cit. i. 124.

'royal prerogative of genius'. Coleridge on the Seventeenth Century, ed. R. F. Brinkley, new edn. (New York, 1968), 546.

'barbaric genius'. The Life of Reason, one-volume edn. (New York, 1954), 311 (*Reason in Art*, ch. 3, 'Emergence of Fine Arts').

'Genius . . . Caliban'. Wyndham Lewis, *The Art of Being Ruled* (London, 1926), 247–9. 'We compose ourselves into a militant league of hatred against the "creative" monster, the inventive brute. Genius has become for us Caliban: what *we* have become, to make this possible, we do not care to consider.'

the *'daimon' . . . kind'. The Letters of D. H. Lawrence*, ed. A. Huxley (New York, 1932), xv, xxix (editor's introduction).

'A happy . . . Nature.' 'Preface of the Translator, with a Parallel, of *Poetry* and Painting', *De Arte Graphica. The Art of Painting*, by C. A. Du Fresnoy, With Remarks, Translated into English . . . by Mr. Dryden (London, 1695), xxxiv.

12 *No, my Lord . . . immortality'. The Letters of John Wilmot, Earl of Rochester*, ed. J. Treglown (Oxford, 1980), 234. See also p. 206 for a note on Blount.

'*Naturall Power . . . Luck.*' *Leviathan*, ed. cit. 150; cf. Macpherson, op. cit. 35.

13 '*whom I . . . Tewkesbury*'. *The Tragedy of Richard III*, I. ii. 240–1(F1).

'*You must . . . serues.*' *Marlowe's Edward II*, ed. W. D. Briggs (London, 1914), 31; contrast *Tamburlaine* (*The Plays of Christopher Marlowe*, ed. R. Gill (Oxford, 1971), 57, Mycetes speech ('I might command you to be slain for this . . .'); Mycetes, 'the witless King' (70), himself an otiosity.

'*Qual . . . morto*'. *Dante's Inferno, with a Translation into English Triple Rhyme by L. Binyon* (London, 1933), 156.

'*I am my selfe alone*'. *The Third Part of Henry the Sixt*, v. vi. 83(F1).

'*What . . . dead*'. Pound, *The Spirit of Romance* (London, 1910), 123.

14 *drafts of the 'Malatesta Cantos'*. See D. Bornstein, 'The Poet as Historian: Researching the Malatesta Cantos', *Paideuma*, 10 (1981), 283–291, at 291. See also M. F. Harper, 'Truth and Calliope: Ezra Pound's Malatesta', *PMLA* 96/1 (Jan. 1981), 86–103.

'*I . . . how it is*'. Pound, *Make it New* (London, 1934), 150–1.

'*Capo . . . end*'). *Dante's Inferno*, ed. cit. 326–7.

'*still gleams . . . acts*'. Ezra Pound, *Selected Prose 1909–1965*, ed. W. Cookson (London, 1973), 169.

'*The Italian . . . personality*'. *Pavannes and Divagations*, 12.

'*Stone . . . Fellow*'. Clarendon, *The History of the Rebellion and Civil Wars in England*, 3 vols. (Oxford, 1702–4), i. 191.

'*We . . . businesse*'. *Brief Lives*, ed. cit. i. 156: from the funeral sermon.

'*vicious . . . Phrase*'. Thomas Sprat, 'History of the Royal Society', in J. E. Spingarn (ed.), *Critical Essays of the Seventeenth Century*, 3 vols. (Oxford, 1908), ii. 117.

'*the ambitious . . . conceaved*'. *Gondibert*, ed. cit. 52 ('The Answer of Mr Hobbes . . .').

'*our stubborne language*'. 'An Elegie upon the death of the Deane of Pauls, Dr Iohn Donne', in *The Poems of Thomas Carew . . .*, ed. R. Dunlap (Oxford, 1949; repr. 1970), 73.

15 '*Poesy*' . . . *Nature)*'. *Gondibert*, ed. cit. 40.

'*The comprehensive . . . Line*'. Spingarn, ed. cit. ii. 298.

'*vultum clausum*'. See *Characters from the Histories and Memoirs of the Seventeenth Century*, ed. D. Nichol Smith (Oxford, 1918), 153.

'*viso . . . Milton. Reliquiae Wottonianae . . .* (London, 1651), 435. Although in this edition the recipient is not named, it was no secret.

Wotton's letter had been made public in Milton's *Poems* of 1645. The date of the letter is 13 Apr. 1638 and Wotton is here repeating advice he had given to an unknown recipient in (possibly) 1636. See *The Life and Letters of Sir Henry Wotton* by L. Pearsall Smith, 2 vols. (Oxford, 1907), ii. 364, 381.

'as free . . . stranger'. Izaac Walton, *The Compleat Angler 1653–1676*, ed. J. Bevan (Oxford, 1983), 63; cf. p. 174.

'not play[ing] . . . life'. *Brief Lives*, ed. cit. ii. 53–4 ('He had not a generall acquaintance').

16 *'To be admitted . . . Service.'* Robert Gould, *Poems Chiefly Consisting of Satyrs and Satyrical Epistles* (London, 1688/9), A4ᵛ.

His poems . . . Estate'. E. H. Sloane, *Robert Gould: Seventeenth Century Satirist* (Philadelphia, 1940), 12–15.

Ezra Pound . . . Bionos. Ed. cit. 147–53; see also Hammond, op. cit. 36–41.

His praise . . . exhausted quite'. *The Poems of John Oldham*, ed. H. F. Brooks and R. Selden (Oxford, 1987), 316, 'To the Memory of . . . Mr. Harman Atwood'.

17 *'inspiration' . . . word'.* *Gondibert*, ed. cit. 22.

'Bagpipe'. Ibid. 49.

'Poetique . . . Age'. *The Poems of John Oldham*, 70; *Remains of Mr. John Oldham in Verse and Prose* (London, 1684), A[1]ᵛ: Thomas Flatman, 'On the Death of Mr. John Oldham. A Pindarique Pastoral Ode'.

'durum . . . share'. Williams, ed. cit. 35. My English rendering is taken from *Virgil with an English translation by H. R. Fairclough*, 2 vols. (Cambridge, Mass., and London, 1978), i. 99.

'whom he had never seen'. *Life*, ed. cit. 253.

Keats . . . Pernambuca'. C. F. E. Spurgeon, *Keats's Shakespeare: A Descriptive Study* (Oxford, 1928), 51.

'They stood . . . fall'. 'Eleanora' was published in 1692. Gould, in 1688/9, had written to, and of, 'Eleanora's' husband: 'Neither are these Showres of Liberality rain'd only on your Domesticks; Strangers, as well as they, have their share' (*Poems*, ed. cit. A4ᵛ).

For, we are fallen . . . people.' *The State of Innocence and Fall of Man: An Opera. Written in Heroique Verse . . . by John Dryden . . .* (London, 1677), b1ᵛ.

18 *'Interests . . . other'.* *Brief Lives*, ed. cit. ii. 72. 'Was not the most magnificent of all replies to Hobbes Milton's *Paradise Lost?*' (M. H. Nicolson, 'Milton and Hobbes', *Studies in Philology*, 23/4

(Oct. 1926), 411). The cogency of this challenge is not diminished by a recognition of complementary elements, as in 'Christ's almost Hobbesian exaggeration of the aristocratic element in the Aristotelian magnanimous man's renunciation of the world' in *Paradise Regain'd*, iii. 47–51. See Carey's note in *Milton: Complete Shorter Poems*, 472.

The legislative style . . . Abdiel. Paradise Lost, v. 805–907. Abdiel's 'flame of zeale' is supremely 'reason'd'; Satan's 'fury' is a cheating 'passion'. It could equally well be said that Dryden's legislative style, like Thomas Sprat's 'Reason set out in plain, undeceiving expressions', is one man's offering towards those unattainable 'united indeavors of some publick minds . . . conversant both in Letters and business' which the proposer for erecting an English Academy envisaged as a 'brave . . . undertaking' in '*Civil History*' and a moral lesson in 'obedience' (see Spingarn, ed. cit. ii. 112, 114–15).

19 '*Princes . . . Heroes*)'. *Gondibert*, ed. cit. 45: 'The Answer of Mr Hobbes.'

2 The Tartar's Bow and the Bow of Ulysses

21 *'Tuneful . . . Song'. Milton's Sonnets*, ed. E. A. J. Honigmann (London, 1966), XIII.

'with . . . accent'. Ibid.

'humor' . . . exigencies'. Ibid. and *The Oxford English Dictionary*, 2nd edn., 20 vols. (Oxford, 1989), xv. 478, xiv. 879, s.v. 'humour', *v.* 2, citing Milton's phrase.

'a . . . style'. Honigmann, ed. cit. 131.

('Thou . . . Quire'). Honigmann, XIII.

Milton's drafts . . . tongue'. John Milton, *Poems*, Reproduced in Facsimile from the Manuscript in Trinity College, Cambridge (Menston, 1970), 43, 45; Honigmann, 126.

22 *'declamatory' . . . no more than this.* For a full discussion see I. Spink, *English Song: Dowland to Purcell* (London, 1974), especially part 1, ch. 2, 'The New Men and the New Music', and part 2, ch. 1, 'Henry Lawes' "tunefull and well measur'd song" '. See also Honigmann, 127–8; *Selected Songs of Thomas Campion*, ed. W. H. Auden and J. Hollander (New York, 1973), 17. I am indebted to Richard Luckett for his advice.

It will . . . 'intolerable'. See R. Peters, *Hobbes* (Harmondsworth, 1956), 17.

23 *'intolerable . . . meanings'.* T. S. Eliot, *Four Quartets* (London, 1944), 17.

Bacon . . . Customes'). *The Twoo Bookes of the Proficience and Advancement of Learning* (London, 1605), Facsimile edn. (Amsterdam and New York, 1970), The second Booke, 57, 56ᵛ.

'attamen . . . sufficiunt'. *The Works of Francis Bacon . . .*, ed. J. Spedding, R. E. Ellis, and D. D. Heath, 7 vols., new edn. (London, 1870), i. 646; iv. 434, 'yet all is not enough'.

'retro . . . retorqueant.' Ibid. ('they shoot back at the understanding from which they proceeded').

24 *'inseparable . . . life'.* *The Twoo Bookes*, ed. cit., The second Booke, 57.

'collective body of assumptions'. Simon Patrick, *A Brief Account of the New Sect of Latitude-Men* (1662), introduction by T. A. Birrell. The Augustan Reprint Society Publication Number 100, (Los Angeles, 1963), iv: Birrell's phrase.

Sir Robert Howard's . . . others'. The Great Favourite Or, The Duke of Lerma (London, 1668), Facsimile edn. (New York, 1975), A4ᵛ, A3.

'providently . . . future'. Peters, 20, citing *English Works*, VIII. vii.

25 *'contexture'.* Citations from *OED*, ed. cit. iii. 821.

Puttenham says . . . man'. The Arte of English Poesie by George Puttenham, ed. G. D. Willcock and A. Walker (Cambridge, 1936), 197.

26 *When Chaucer . . . Nicholas'. The Works of Geoffrey Chaucer*, ed. F. N. Robinson, 2nd edn. (London, 1957), 44 (line 2779), 48 (line 3204).

'Measure' . . . short'. Ed. cit. 67.

In Skelton's . . . merry'. Magnyfycence . . . by John Skelton, ed. R. L. Ramsay (Early English Text Society, Extra Series, 98; London, 1908; repr. 1958), 4–5 ('wylde Insolence', 'I ponder . . . wrought'), liii ('so-called tumbling verse'), lxviii ('macaronic hexameter'), xiii ('a notable shortcoming . . . is the character-drawing'), 22–3 ('To passe . . . perylous thynge'). 1 ('A goodly . . . merry'). See also xlii: 'It would seem that Skelton prided himself especially on the invention and delineation of this little group of typical evil courtiers [i.e. Counterfet Countenance, Crafty Conueyaunce, Clokyd Colusyon, Courtly Abusyon]'. R. S. Kinsman suggests, in his introduction to *John Skelton: Poems* (Oxford, 1969), that 'Skelton . . . seeks metrically to distinguish the characters of his play' (x). In the quoted passage I adopt Ramsay's punctuation and capitals but retain Rastell's(?) unindented line-setting.

27 *Wyatt's . . . deserued.* The editorial problems presented by Wyatt's poems are notorious. See the exhaustive discussion of textual questions in H. A. Mason's *Editing Wyatt* (Cambridge, 1972) and *Sir Thomas Wyatt: A Literary Portrait* (Bristol, 1986). My reading is indebted to R. Harrier, *The Canon of . . . Wyatt's Poetry* (Cambridge, Mass., 1975), 131–2 (I have removed the MS contractions from 'serued', 'deserued'). Harrier transcribes from the Egerton MS; Mason argues for the superiority of the Devonshire text's markedly different reading of the final line. See also K. Muir (ed.), *The Life and Letters of Sir Thomas Wyatt* (Liverpool, 1963), 146, 164, 166, 168; W. Tydeman (ed.), *English Poetry 1400–1580* (London, 1970), 220, 19.

28 *'haughty . . . serfs'. The Ancrene Riwle* (The Corpus MS: *Ancrene Wisse*), Translated into Modern English by M. B. Salu (London, 1955), 158. In Middle English: '& þolieð ofte danger of swuch oðerhwile þe mahte beon ower þreal' (*Ancrene Wisse*, Parts Six and Seven, ed. G. Shepherd (London and Edinburgh, 1959), 7).

newfangleness. In Chaucer, e.g. 'The Squire's Tale', line 610: 'Men loven of propre kynde newefangelnesse, | As briddes doon that men in cages fede.'

In Arcite's death-speech. See N. Coghill, 'Chaucer's Idea of What is Noble', *English Association Presidential Address* (1971), 13. Coghill observes that in these lines Chaucer is free from the influence of Boccaccio, the author to whom 'The Knight's Tale' is elsewhere much indebted.

29 *'a figure . . . away'. The Garden of Eloquence (1593)* by Henry Peacham, A Facsimile Reproduction with an Introduction by W. G. Crane (Gainesville, 1954), 56.

Puttenham . . . 'reproue'. The Arte of English Poesie, ed. cit. 202–3. But Puttenham appears to conflate *'Prosonomasia,* or the Nicknamer' (A by-name geuen in sport', as 'Errans mus' for 'Erasmus') with *paronomasia* (*OED,* 'after παρονομάξειν to alter slightly in naming.], a playing on words which sound alike; a word-play, a pun'). The compiler of the 1589 'table' or index complicates matters further by referring to 'Paronomasia, *or the nicknamer'* (ed. cit. 312). Angel Day, in *The English Secretorie* (1586), also 'confused' the two terms (see *OED,* s.v. 'Prosonomasia').

'vnkyndly'. Tottel's Miscellany (1557–1587), ed. H. E. Rollins, 2 vols. (Cambridge, Mass., 1929), i. 39 (No. 52).

The seventh chapter . . . courtiers'. Ed. cit. 154–5.

'ornament poeticall'. Ibid. 137.

'the spacious . . . diuision'. I allude to Troilus's speech on the defection of Cressida, in Shakespeare's play (v. ii. 137–60, at 150), to which later reference is made (text as First Folio [*F1*]).

30 *'I doute not . . . iudgmente'.* Wyatt: *Life and Letters,* 189.

'but one . . . chaynged'. Ibid. 197.

'[W]hat . . . thynges?' Ibid. 203.

Puttenham . . . interpretation of words. Ed. cit. xxxviii, xviii.

'real . . . suffering'. Preface to *Lyrical Ballads,* in *The Poetical Works of William Wordsworth,* ed. E. De Selincourt, 4 vols. (Oxford, 1944), ii. 394: 'However exalted a notion we would wish to cherish of the character of a Poet, it is obvious, that while he describes and imitates passions, his employment is in some degree mechanical, compared with the freedom and power of real and substantial action and suffering.'

'figures rhethoricall'. Puttenham, ed. cit. 196.

'practisis' and 'trafiques'. Wyatt, *Life and Letters*, 127–8.

31 *'DISPUTANDI . . . CHURCH'. Reliquiae Wottonianae . . .* (London, 1651), c8ᵛ.

'morall Images, and Examples'. Sir Fulke Greville's Life of Sir Philip Sidney etc. First Published 1652, with an Introduction by Nowell Smith (Oxford, 1907), 223.

'the "fleering . . . nose" '. Ed. cit. lxxxii.

'fain[ing]'. The Works of Thomas Nashe, ed. R. B. McKerrow, corrected reprint, 5 vols. (Oxford, 1966), i. 183.

'Ovt . . . selfe?' Ibid.

'iesting'. Ibid. 209.

'Cum autem . . . rebel']. Bacon, *Works*, ed. cit. i. 645; iv. 433.

32 *'You . . . time.'* J. Rathbone, 'A Pianist as Violinist', *Tempo: A Quarterly Review of Modern Music*, 123 (Dec. 1977), 14–22, at 21.

Two . . . alone. The Poems and Letters of Andrew Marvell, ed. H. M. Margoliouth, 3rd edn., rev. P. Legouis and E. E. Duncan-Jones, 2 vols. (Oxford, 1971), i. 53.

'dissections . . . Word. Essays in Divinity by John Donne, ed. E. M. Simpson (Oxford, 1952), 57. There is a beautiful enactment of the pains of cribration in Newman's letter to his sister Jemima, 29 Jan. 1838. It is of course true that 'Newman customarily used little dashes, to do duty for a comma, a semi-colon or a full stop, when he was writing informally and at speed' (*A Packet of Letters: A Selection from the Correspondence of John Henry Newman*, ed. J. Sugg (Oxford, 1983), xxi, editor's introduction) but in this letter the customary device is made a parody of itself and of the various pressures which make it necessary. The plethoric 'little dash' suggests both unremitting activity and continuous agitation ('—I put it by—I take it up—I begin to correct again—it will not do—alterations multiply—pages are re-written—little lines sneak in and crawl about—') while taking comic advantage of both; it is as if the 'dashes' were themselves dashing away with the smoothing-iron. The charm of the passage is chiefly due to the fact that Newman does, after all, most effectively reduce the 'business' to 'a very homely undertaking': 'washing a sponge of the sea gravel and sea smell' (op. cit. 43).

'this examination . . . Saviours.' The Sermons of John Donne, ed. G. R. Potter and E. M. Simpson, 10 vols. (Berkeley and Los Angeles, 1953–62), x. 247.

33 *In a letter . . . power.* The sermon 'Preached to the King, at White-Hall, the first of April, 1627': *Sermons*, ed. cit. vii. 39–40, 393. R. C. Bald,

John Donne: A Life (London, 1970), 525 n. 1, suggests that, as a result of the trouble caused by this sermon, it may have become Donne's habit thereafter 'to write out his Court sermons in full'.

If I say . . . speech. One observes that 'heft' itself may sustain a subtle tuning, as in Whitman's 'Hefts of the moving world at innocent gambols silently rising, freshly exuding' ('Song of Myself', line 553) or Emily Dickinson's 'There's a certain Slant of light, | Winter Afternoons — | That oppresses, like the Heft | Of Cathedral Tunes—' (*The Complete Poems of Emily Dickinson*, ed. T. H. Johnson (London, 1975), 118). One observes further that received tuning-words may be satirically subjected to violent hefts, as in Nashe's 'Hence, double diligence, thou mean'st deceit' (*Svmmers Last Will and Testament*, 1163; see *Works*, iii. 270) or in Jonson's 'the *Senate's* brainlesse diligence' (*Seianus*, iii. 472; see *Ben Jonson*, ed. C. H. Herford and P. Simpson, 11 vols. (Oxford, 1925–52), iv. 408). Anthony Lane draws my attention to a passage in C. S. Peirce (see *Collected Papers of Charles Sanders Peirce*, ed. C. Hartshorne, P. Weiss, *et al.*, 8 vols. Cambridge, Mass., 1931–58), vi. 217): '. . . It is not in perceiving its qualities that they know it, but in hefting its insistency then and there, which Duns called its *haecceitas*—or, if he didn't, it was this that he was groping after . . .' I understand 'its . . . its . . . its' to refer to 'every correlate of an existential relation' posited in a previous sentence. Although 'hefting' strikes one as having been chosen with a degree of expressive care, 'It is not . . .' and 'it was this . . .' appear as lax and intrusive locutions in a statement which lays a heavy semantic burden on 'it'. Metaphysically deft and resonant ('hefting its insistency then and there . . .'), syntactically both strained and slack, Peirce's sentence embodies the positive and negative aspects of word-hefting.

'such as may serve . . . are so'. John Locke, *An Essay . . .*, ed. cit. 476, 492.

'unsteady . . . Notions'. Ibid. 492.

34 *'being true . . . uncertaine'.* The Works of George Herbert, ed. F. E. Hutchinson (Oxford, 1941), 264–5.

'just occasion'. Ibid. 265.

'divine . . . vertue'. Ibid. 267.

'Since . . . Musique'. John Donne, *The Divine Poems*, ed. H. Gardner (Oxford, 1952), 50.

'I am . . . sit.' Ibid. 44.

35 *'I returned . . . patronage of you'.* Poems and Letters, ii. 81.

In the lyric dialogues . . . 1650s. See e.g. D. M. Friedman, *Marvell's Pastoral Art* (Berkeley, Calif., 1970), 2, 33 n. 11.

'*busie Companies of Men*'. *Poems and Letters*, i. 51.

'*really . . . you*'. Ibid. ii. 42.

36 '*precious Time*' . . . *Colen*' *etc.*). Ibid. ii. 323–5.

'*Civill . . . House*'. *The Sermons of John Donne*, ed. cit. iii. 361, 'Preached at Saint Pauls upon Christmasse day, 1621'; *The Diary of Samuel Pepys, A New and Complete Transcription*, ed. R. Latham and W. Matthews, 11 vols. (London, 1970–83), vii. 24; Marvell, *Poems and Letters*, ii. 52, 44, 23.

'*The Ballast . . . businesse*'. *Poems and Letters*, ii. 33, 61.

as Sir Henry Wotton observes . . . tacite'. *The Life and Letters of Sir Henry Wotton*, ed. L. P. Smith, 2 vols. (Oxford, 1907), ii. 15.

'*My L: Mordants . . . Chatham*'. *Poems and Letters*, ii. 53, 60.

'*You are not ignorant of our Business with you*'. *Amboyna*, A Tragedy . . . Written by John Dryden . . . (London, 1673), 54.

'*my Tanger=Boates business*'. *Diary*, ed. cit. vii. 24. See also vi. 146, 172, 286; xi, 278–9.

'*For the Moral . . . Poet.*' Du Fresnoy, *The Art of Painting*, ed. cit. xix ('Preface of the Translator . . .').

37 '*'tis your business . . . here*'. Dryden, *Poems*, ed. Kinsley, 39.

'*thus fell . . . innocence*'. *Characters from the Histories and Memoirs of the Seventeenth Century*, ed. D. Nichol Smith (Oxford, 1918), 86.

'*For, this life . . . businesse*'. John Donne, *Sermons*, ed. cit. viii. 53.

('*Make you . . . will*'). Epistle to the Hebrews, 13: 21 (as 1611).

'*Domestique . . . practice*'. Greville, ed. cit. 185, 211. The 'ideal' model for the integration of 'domestic affairs' with the common weal is given in book II, ch. 3, of More's *Utopia*: 'Therfore matters of greate weyghte and importaunce he brought to the electyon house of the syphograuntes, whyche open the matter to their familyes; and afterwarde, when they haue consulted among them selfes, they shewe their deuyse to the cowncell' (*The Utopia of Sir Thomas More . . .*, ed. J. H. Lupton (Oxford, 1895), 137). For the cohabitation of ideal and unideal in the Tudor Court see E. W. Ives's discussion, *Anne Boleyn* (Oxford, 1986), ch. 1: 'More himself was well aware that in the real world of the Renaissance court, the best that morality and honesty could hope to achieve was compromise. How difficult that was, his own future career would show' (9). For a figurative application see Milton, *The Tenure of Kings and Magistrates*: '. . . to dispose and *oeconomize* in the Land which God hath giv'n them, as Maisters of

Family in thir own house and free inheritance' (C. A. Patrides (ed.), *John Milton: Selected Prose* (Harmondsworth, 1974), 280).

'Poetical' . . . *not 'reall'*. Greville, ed. cit. 46.

'safe . . . *duty'*. Ibid. 126. Dryden's poetic and dramatic 'interest in the limits of maxims' has been suggested by Alan Fisher: 'The maxims of rational control are true, they are wise, and they apply—but there is no *power* in them: they cannot save one from the forces of life.' See *New Homage to John Dryden: Papers Read at a Clark Library Conference Feb. 13–14 1981*, by P. Harth, A. Fisher, and R. Cohen, with an Introduction by A. Roper (Los Angeles, 1983), 38, 42.

38 *'buisinesses* . . . *accidents'*. Ed. cit. ii. 96; collated with the original manuscript held in the Public Record Office, London (SP99, Bundle 21, fo. 124).

'insolent' . . . *'devourers'*. Homer: *The Odyssey*, with an English Translation by A. T. Murray, 2 vols. (London and New York, 1919), ii. 275, 267.

'aptnesse' and 'cunnynge'. Roger Ascham, *English Works*, ed. W. A. Wright (Cambridge, 1904), 62.

'I never . . . *Cleopatra'*. *The Art of Painting*, ed. cit. liv.

'Con Amore . . . *it selfe'*. *Of the Elements of Architecture: The Second Part.* This is included in *Reliquiae Wottonianae*, 1651; see p. 274.

39 *'Instantly* . . . *not.'* 'The American Scholar', in *Essays and Lectures*, ed. J. Porte (New York, 1983), 60.

3   Caveats Enough in their Own Walks

41   *An apophthegm of Cicero.* See *Cicero's Letters to Atticus*, ed. D. R. Shackleton Bailey, 7 vols. (Cambridge, 1965–70), i. 198–9.

'learned men' . . . walkes'. The Twoo Bookes of the Proficience and Advancement of Learning (London, 1605), Facsimile edn. (Amsterdam and New York, 1970), The first Booke, 14.

'did believe . . . indulgent'. Characters from the Histories and Memoirs of the Seventeenth Century, ed. D. Nichol Smith (Oxford, 1918), 95.

'the common practice of men'. Ibid. 94.

42   *He wrote frequently . . . of the whole Businesse'. Wotton*, ed. L. P. Smith (collated, as indicated, with the original manuscripts held in the Public Record Office and in the British Library), ii. 42 (PRO, SP84, vol. 70, fo. 58), ii. 50 (SP84, vol. 70, fo. 122), ii. 56 (BL Stowe MS175, fo. 71).

'one maine knott in the whole businesse'. ii. 191 (*Letters and Dispatches from Sir Henry Wotton to James I and his Ministers*, Printed from the Originals in the Library of Eton College (Roxburghe Club (London, 1850), 223).

'tyme to knitt knotts'. ii. 96 (PRO, SP99, Bundle 21, fol. 124).

'ballance' . . . duty'. Sir Fulke Greville's Life of Sir Philip Sidney etc. First Published 1652, with an Introduction by Nowell Smith (Oxford, 1907), 126.

43   *'holding a meane . . . equiuocation'*. ii. 251 (SP99, Bundle 24, fo. 190ᵛ).

'Policie' . . . 'most immersed'. Twoo Bookes, ed. cit., The second Booke, 64.

'that which taketh . . . Generalities'. Ibid.

'Macciauell . . . do'. Ibid., The second Booke, 77.

The ancient . . . renown. The Annals of Tacitus, ed. H. Furneaux, 2 vols. (Oxford, 1884), i. (2nd edn., 1896), 483–5.

44   *Seneca . . . proscripsit.'* Seneca, *Moral Essays*, with an English Translation by J. W. Basore, 3 vols. (London and New York, 1932), ii. 90–1: 'in which he himself proscribed for all time the agents of proscription' (I have changed 'sponsors' to 'agents').

'the wit . . . thereby'. Op. cit., The first Booke, 20.

'diligent . . . creatures'. Ibid., The first Booke, 22.

45 *'Every . . . season.'* Ecclesiastes 3: 11, 'He hath made euery thing beautifull in his time' (The Bible of 1611).

Bacon . . . pleasure. See The first Booke, 4.

Clarendon . . . eare'. Characters . . ., 95.

Aubrey . . . bussinesse'. Aubrey's Brief Lives, ed. O. L. Dick (Harmondsworth, 1972), 233. Clark 'suppressed' this phrase in his edition of 1898 (see i. 188).

'convivium . . . theologicum'. *Characters. . . .*, 92.

Aldrovandus . . . fishes . . . The second Edition much enlarged (London, 1655), 178. This was the first appearance of the passage. See Bevan, ed. cit. 272–3, for the 1676 reading, which differs in small details.

46 *George Wither's . . . matter'. The Hymns and Songs of the Chvrch . . . Translated, and Composed by G.W.* (London, 1623), A2, A2^v.

'To this . . . mediocrity'. The Sermons of John Donne, ed. G. R. Potter and E. M. Simpson, 10 vols. (Berkeley and Los Angeles, 1953–62), viii. 88–9. It was a familiar reproach that the disguised Jesuit mission-priests went about in costly ostentatious attire. Southwell defended the practice, as being framed 'to the necessity of our daies'. 'It is noe sure Argument of inward vanity to be vaine in shew, sith a modest and an humble mynd may be shrowded vnder the glorious and Courtly Robes of a vertuous *Hester*' (*An Humble Supplication to Her Maiestie by Robert Southwell* (1591), ed. R. C. Bald (Cambridge, 1953), 8, 8 n.2, 9).

'generous . . . men'. Characters . . ., 77.

Wither . . . easier way. Ed. cit. A2^v.

Walton's . . . what it may seem. An impression substantiated by the textual history of this very phrase: 'the most honest, ingenious, harmless Art of Angling', 1653; 'the most *honest, ingenuous, quiet,* and *harmless* art of *Angling*', 1676. See Bevan, ed. cit. 69, 193. See also below, p. 125.

The Life . . . Wottonianae. D. Novarr, *The Making of Walton's 'Lives'* (Ithaca, NY, 1958), ch. 5, provides a useful commentary on significant verbal changes in the three editions of *Reliquiae* issued during Walton's lifetime.

47 *'Old fashioned Poetry, but choicely good'.* It may be worth noting that Walton also uses 'choicely good' to commend carps' tongues: Bevan, ed. cit. 130.

In the third edition of 1661. 76.

But 'strong lines . . . obscurity'. Sir William Davenant's Gondibert, ed. D. F. Gladish (Oxford, 1971), 52, 'The Answer of Mr Hobbes'. See also G. Williamson, *Seventeenth Century Contexts* (London, 1960), 120–31.

At this . . . bite'. Wotton, ed. Smith, ii. 20 (*Letters of Sir Henry Wotton to Sir Edmund Bacon* (London, 1661), 160). One may add: '. . . having in the meane tyme like the fishermen of thease lagune only prepared owre netts and owre hookes to catche somewhat heereafter', ii. 97–8 (SP99, Bundle 21, fo. 141).

added to the second edition. Bevan, ed. cit. 49.

48 *as though floating . . . maxims.* The kind of *tone* I have in mind is 'Per il che si ha notare che gli uomini si debbono o vezzeggiare o spegnere', Englished by Dacres as 'for it is to be noted, that men must either be dallied and flatterd withall, or else be quite crusht'. see *Il Principe . . .*, ed. L. A. Burd (Oxford, 1891), 188–9; *The Prince . . . Reprinted from the Translation by Edward Dacres published in 1640* (London, 1929), 9.

'reciprocall . . . duties'. Greville, op. cit. 180.

'To come . . . power'. King Lear, i. i. 170 (*Q1–2*: 'betweene').

('Huddled . . . Convenience'). The Metaphysical Poets, ed. H. Gardner, revised edn. (Harmondsworth, 1966), 222.

'But Fate . . . betwixt'. The Poems and Letters of Andrew Marvell, ed. H. M. Margoliouth, 3rd edn., rev. P. Legouis and E. E. Duncan-Jones, 2 vols. (Oxford, 1971), i. 39.

49 *Nor did . . . spent'.* cf. *Compleat Angler,* ed. Bevan, 76.

Pound's . . . translate'. Literary Essays of Ezra Pound, ed. T. S. Eliot (London, 1954), 25.

Bacon's caveat . . . really are. The Twoo Bookes, ed. cit., The first Booke, 19. I also quote Spedding's gloss (iii. 285 n. 1) on Bacon's augmented Latin version (i. 452): 'delicias et lauticias.'

'And you must Fish for him with a strong Line'. Third edition (1661), 127.

50 *According to Walton's . . . note.* See Novarr, op. cit. 160.

'stretched sinews' . . . 'art'. Works, ed. cit. 41, 'Easter'.

'crabbed . . . syntax'. John Donne, *The Satires, Epigrams and Verse Letters,* ed. W. Milgate (Oxford, 1967), 228 (editorial commentary).

Donne engineers . . . self-purification. Cf. ibid. 223 (editorial commentary).

51 *'As Walton observed . . . this voyage'.* Donne's wounded ambition and Walton's brisk parenthetical tact are equally concerned with Donne's self-blighted career, the disgrace and loss of worldly prospects incurred by his secret marriage to Ann More. See R. C. Bald, *John Donne: A Life* ed. cit. 128, 145–6.

52 *'the painfull . . . Vertue'. Gondibert*, ed. cit. 14.

Such words . . . circumstances. In the 'Preface' to *The Elements of Architecture* Wotton expands upon the sentiment of the letter from Venice: '. . . I have born abroad some part of his [the King's] *civil* Service; yet when I came home, and was again resolved into mine own simplicity, I found it fitter for my *Penne* (at least in this first publique adventure) to deale with these plain *Compilements*, and tractable *Materials*; then with the *Laberynths* and *Mysteries* of *Courts* and *States*' (*Reliquiae Wottonianae* (1651), 198).

The Rt. Hon. H. H. Asquith . . . Bohemia" '. *Sir Henry Wotton, with some General Reflections on Style in English Poetry* (English Association Pamphlets, 44; Presidential Address 1919), 3, 7, 8, 6.

53 *[W]ritten . . . remembered. Wotton*, ed. Smith, i. 170–1.

'ordinary . . . Life'. Locke, *Essay . . .*, ed. cit. 492.

54 *written in 1619 or 1620 . . . Petrarch.* Asquith, op. cit. 7, suggests 1619; for 1620 see *Wotton*, ed. Smith, i. 170–1 n. 1, ii. 415.

'forraign imployments . . . Nation'. Compleat Angler, ed. Bevan, 76.

You meaner Beauties . . . shall rise? This is a notoriously 'eclectic' text. I accept the argument, and adopt the reading, of J. B. Leishman, ' "You meaner Beauties of the Night": A Study in Transmission and Transmogrification', *The Library*, 26/2–3 (1945), 99–121.

55 *'Jewell of Diamonds . . . pleas'd he should call her'.* These revisions are noted in Novarr, op. cit., 175–7.

Wotton . . . practice of the time. Wotton, ed. Smith, i. 174 n. 3.

'great dexteritie . . . conceyte'. Ibid. i., 354 (SP99, Bundle 3, fo. 108).

'rich Iewel . . . deare'. I. v. 46–7 (text as First Folio).

56 *'points of conuenience . . . stato'. The Twoo Bookes*, ed. cit., The first Booke, 9.

Machiavelli's . . . e le cose'. Il Principe, ed. cit., 190, 246, 361.

'affayres of the world'. The Prince . . . (1640), ed. cit. 48.

'A peece . . . curiositie'. Wotton, ed. Smith, ii. 147; Roxburghe, 34.

('I call . . . occupation'). Wotton, ed. Smith, i. 351 (SP99, Bundle 3, fo. 88).

'how wholeheartedly . . . profession'. Ibid. i. 66.

57 *'enter'd into . . . matter'.* Letters to Lord Zouch, 8 May 1592., 21 Apr. 1591 (*Reliquiae Wottonianae*, The Fourth Edition . . . (London, 1685), 651, 649).

Among Plutarch's Moralia. Plutarch's *Moralia* with an English Translation by F. C. Babbitt, 14 vols. (London, 1928), ii. 4–41: 'How to Profit by one's Enemies.'

Of the Benefit . . . Enemies. The Works of Henry Vaughan, ed. L. C. Martin, 2 vols. (Oxford, 1914), i. 97–108.

'Where our . . . our selves.' Ibid. 103.

'vitious unfolding . . . errours'. Ibid. 104.

'so ingenuous . . .' Thus, in editions of 1651 (c2) and 1654 (47); 'so ingenious', 1672 (c6). Cf. above, p. 122.

Pliny the Elder's discourse. In *Nat. Hist* xxxiv. 9–19.

58 *'quas ne victor quidem abolevit'. Annals*, ed. cit. (Furneaux), i. 532. See also Tacitus, *Histories/Annals*, trans. C. H. Moore and J. Jackson, 4 vols. (London and New York, 1937), iii. 62–3.

exercised in discreet privacy. Annals, ed. Furneaux, ii (2nd edn., revised, 1907), 436–7. See also Pliny, *Letters*, trans. W. Melmoth, 2 vols. (London and New York, 1915), i. 58–61).

'adulatio' ['servile flattery'] and 'avaritia'. Annals, i. 180, 182. See also *The Annals of Tacitus*, Books 1–6, ed. F. R. D. Goodyear, vol. i (Cambridge, 1972), 97.

It is a piece of unassimilated matter lodged in the body politic. I here allude to my own earlier argument, in 'Our Word is Our Bond'. See *The Lords of Limit* (London, 1984), 143.

flagitia. Annals, i. 652. See also *Histories/Annals*, ed. cit. iii. 238–9.

'verba . . . permodesto'. Annals, i. 189. See also Goodyear, ed. cit. 139–40.

59 *'words . . . reueng'd'. Ben Jonson*, ed. cit. iv. 407, line 445.

'meta-theology' . . . divines'. Op. cit. 59, 129 (Simpson's notes). In the *OED* (1933), vi. 377, Donne's usage (*ante* 1615) is the sole citation. In the second edition (1989), ix. 662, Donne remains the single example of this sense (*a*). However, there is now a sense (*b*) = the philosophical study of the nature of religious language or statements. The *OED* (1989) gives three citations for (*b*) (1957, 1959, 1967), and records the derivations 'meta-theologian' (1967) and 'meta-theological' (1969). It is perhaps necessary to remark that, when I speak of 'meta-poetry', I do not mean 'the philosophical study of the nature of poetic language or statements'.

'mis-interpretable . . . Ostentation'. Essayes in Divinity, 59.

There is a letter . . . resist them.' John Donne, *Paradoxes and Problems*, ed. H. Peters (Oxford, 1980), xxv–xxvi and xxv n. 2 ('General

Introduction'); R. C. Bald, *John Donne: A Life*, ed. cit. 121 and n. 1; John Donne, *Selected Prose*, chosen by E. Simpson, edited by H. Gardner and T. Healy (Oxford, 1967), 111.

('When thou hast done . . .'). *The Divine Poems*, ed. cit. 51.

'they have beene written . . . [truth].' *Selected Prose*, 111.

('But what thynge . . . suche thynges'). *The Life and Letters of Sir Thomas Wyatt*, ed. K. Muir (Liverpool, 1963), 203.

('There is⁻nothing . . . peruert'). *The Works of Thomas Nashe*, ed. R. B. McKerrow, corrected reprint, 5 vols. (Oxford, 1966), i. 154.

61 *'the short and sure precepts of good example'*. *Discourses upon Seneca the Tragedian* (1601), by Sir William Cornwallis, Facsimile Reproduction with an Introduction by R. H. Bowers (Gainesville, Fla., 1952), G4.

4 Dryden's Prize-Song

63 *'to judge rightly . . . performance'. Johnson Prose and Poetry,* ed. M. Wilson (London, 1966), 857–8.

64 *'intelligence at bay'. Selected Prose 1909–1965,* ed. W. Cookson (London, 1973), 386.

65 *''tis not necessary . . . Taste'. The Great Favourite, Or, The Duke of Lerma* (London, 1668), Facsimile edn. (New York, 1975), A3, 'To the Reader'. See H. Trowbridge, 'The Place of Rules in Dryden's Criticism', *Modern Philology,* 44 (1946–7), 84–96, esp. pp. 86–7.

Ruskin . . . value. The Works of John Ruskin, ed. E. T. Cook and A. Wedderburn, 38 vols. (London, 1903–12). See e.g. xvii. 164, xviii. 391, xxvii. 217.

Pound . . . egotism'. Selected Prose, 34.

'graded . . . word'. Pound, *Guide to Kulchur,* 3rd impression (London, 1960), 317.

'literature . . . meaning'. ABC of Reading (London, 1951), 28.

66 *'voudriez vous . . . legions?' Les Essais de Michel de Montaigne,* ed. P. Villey (Paris, 1965), 921: livre III, chapitre vii, 'De l'Incommodité de la Grandeur'.

'Neither . . . disallowed.' The Twoo Bookes of the Proficience and Advancement of Learning (London, 1605), Facsimile edn. (Amsterdam and New York, 1970), The first Booke, 17.

in Florio's English version of it. The Essayes of Michael Lord of Montaigne Done into English by John Florio (1603), 3 vols. (London, 1908), iii. 190.

67 *'brute' . . . 'actuality'. Collected Papers of Charles Sanders Peirce,* ed. C. Hartshorne, P. Weiss, *et al.,* 8 vols. (Cambridge, Mass, 1931–58), i. 7 (from the Lowell Lectures of 1903). See also *Semiotic and Significs: The Peirce–Welby Correspondence,* ed. C. S. Hardwick (Indiana UP, 1977), 26 (letter of 12 Oct. 1904); C. S. Peirce, 'A Neglected Argument for the Reality of God', *The Hibbert Journal,* 7 (Oct. 1908–July 1909), 90–112, at 91.

'nothing . . . manœuvre'. J. C. Ransom, *The World's Body,* paperback edn. (Baton Rouge, 1968), 211.

'the necessity . . . audience'. E. Pechter, *Dryden's Classical Theory of Literature* (Cambridge, 1975), 106.

'Voulez-vous . . . fictions?' Nicolas Boileau-Despréaux, *L'Art poétique*, in Boileau, *Œuvres complètes*, introduction by A. Adam, Text and Notes by F. Escal (Paris, 1966), 158, 169, 174, 182. Cf. Pechter, op. cit. 67–8.

Joel Spingarn's notion. Critical Essays of the Seventeenth Century, 3 vols. (Oxford, 1908), i, p. xciii.

68 *'admirable . . . Spectateurs'.* L'Abbé d'Aubignac, *La Pratique du théâtre*, ed. Martino (Algiers and Paris, 1927), 38.

'La tourbe . . . d'inconstance.' Ed. cit. 624: livre II, chapitre xvi, 'De la Gloire'.

'au peuple . . . à contenter'. Ibid. 918.

'N'offrez . . . plaire'. Boileau, Ed. cit. 159.

Montaigne . . . 'la tourbe'. P. Burke, *Montaigne* (New York, 1981), 4–6; F. S. Brown, *Religious and Political Conservatism in the 'Essais' of Montaigne* (Geneva, 1963), 75.

69 *Dryden . . . freedom.* G. McFadden, *Dryden the Public Writer 1660–1685* (Princeton, 1978), 43.

'Les autres . . . moy mesme.' Ed. cit. 657–8: livre II, chapitre xvii, 'De la Praesumption'.

'to write . . . honour. A. Nicoll, *A History of English Drama 1660–1900*, i. *Restoration Drama 1660–1700*, 4th edn. (Cambridge, 1952), 328; Ward, op. cit. 57.

70 *In the end . . . measure'.* C. E. Ward, *The Life of John Dryden* (Chapel Hill, 1961), 302.

'Que toûjours . . . Rime'. Ed. cit. 157. C. S. Peirce calls *bon sens* 'a pretty phrase for ineradicable prejudice'. See *Values in a Universe of Chance: Selected Writings of Charles S. Peirce (1839–1914)*, ed. P. P. Wiener (Stanford, Calif., 1958), 269.

One hears . . . shuffling'. E.g. D. Griffin, 'Dryden's "Oldham" and the Perils of Writing', *MLQ* 37 (1976), 146; R. Salvaggio, *Dryden's Dualities* (Victoria, BC, 1983), 60, 61, 66; N. Jose, 'Dryden and Other Selves', *The Critical Review*, 25 (1983), 111.

the 'position . . . quarters'. The *Oxford English Dictionary*, 2nd edn., 20 vols. (Oxford, 1989), i. 1016.

71 *an attack by the Earl of Rochester.* See Ward, op. cit. 109, 126.

Jean Segrais. See 'The Dedication of the Aeneis', in Dryden, *Poems,* ed. cit. 1051–2, 2046.

72 *Davenant's argument . . . labour'. Gondibert*, ed. cit. 24, 22.

73 *"Tis not . . . Bubbles'. The Spanish Fryar: Or, The Double Discovery . . . Written by Mr. Dryden* (London, 1695), A2ᵛ. ('The Epistle Dedicatory').

Rochester's . . . sneers. See Ward, *Life*, ed. cit. 182; M. van Doren, *John Dryden: A Study of his Poetry*, 3rd edn. (New York, 1946), 28.

'prevailing . . . procedure'. OED, ed. cit. vi. 444, s.v. 'genius', 3*c*.

Eliot . . . nebula'. Homage to John Dryden: Three Essays on Poetry of the Seventeenth Century (London, 1924), 22, 23; *John Dryden, Poet, Dramatist, Critic* (New York, 1932), 34.

74 *Auden . . . say'. A Choice of Dryden's Verse* (London, 1973), 9.

One of Dryden's . . . Marcellus. Anon., 'Damon, an Eclogue on the untimely Death of Mr. Oldham', in *Remains of Mr. John Oldham in Verse and Prose* (London, 1684), A5ᵛ. Noted by Griffin, op. cit. 148 n. 35.

75 *'blooming Ripeness' . . . Habitude'. The Poems of John Oldham*, 292–3.

'Rich . . . Knave'. Ibid. 199, 224.

In November 1684 . . . fifty-fourth year. He was born on 9 Aug. 1631.

and had been Poet Laureate . . . Rochester. See Ward, *Life*, 56, 186; *Poems*, ed. Kinsley, 1955; P. Hammond, *John Oldham and the Renewal of Classical Culture* (Cambridge, 1983), 19, 29–30.

It has been suggested . . . emotions. T. H. Fujimura, 'The Personal Element in Dryden's Poetry', *PMLA* 89 (1974), 1007–23 at 1010.

'capricious . . . hatred'. Ward, *Life*, 83.

Dryden . . . afterwards. See the letter from Rochester in the country to Henry Savile in London, spring 1676: '. . . You write me word that I'm out of favour with a certain poet whom I have ever admired for the disproportion of him and his attributes.' Treglown associates this remark with Dryden's anger at Rochester's gibes in 'An Allusion to Horace' written in the winter of 1675–6. *The Letters of John Wilmot, Earl of Rochester*, ed. J. Treglown (Oxford, 1980), 119–20; Dryden's letter to Rochester some three years earlier (Apr.–May 1673) had been entirely amiable. 'The reasons for Rochester's change are far from clear, though possibly the Earl of Mulgrave's patronage of Dryden, from 1674 or 1675 onwards, contributed to Rochester's disaffection': *The Letters of John Dryden*, ed. C. E. Ward (Durham, NC, 1942), 145 (editorial commentary).

76 *'At about . . . satire.* Hammond, op. cit. 30, 63–5.

Oldham's Satyrs . . . print. For the date 1680–1 see *The Poems of John Oldham*, p. xxxiii; on the other points see pp. xlvii, civ n. 81. See also Hammond, op. cit. 86, 218; Ward, *Life*, 167.

and other poets . . . 1682. Poems, ed. Kinsley, 1913–14.

'indulgent'. Dryden's word for Aeneas, book v, line 470; discussed by Griffin, op. cit. 138–9.

77 *'Thus Nisus fell . . . race together into death.* Twelve or thirteen years before the publication, in 1697, of the *Aeneis* Dryden had translated the Nisus and Euryalus episodes from books v and ix. These were included in *Sylvae* (1685). It is therefore highly probable that the composition of 'To the Memory of Mr Oldham' (1684) coincided with Dryden's work on these passages, which are the ground upon which the elegy builds its solemn descant. See *Poems*, ed. Kinsley, 1180–4 and 1294–307, for collation of 1685 and 1697. See also Hammond, op. cit. 208–16.

The Latin . . . 'sed . . .' See *The Aeneid of Virgil*, ed. R. D. Williams, 2 vols. (London, 1972–3), i. 107 (book v, lines 332–3).

('venerande . . . ambo!'). Aeneid, ed. cit. ii. 58, 64 (book ix, lines 276, 446).

('sed nox . . . umbra'). Aeneid, ed. cit. i. 152 (book vi, line 866).

'sed pronus . . . cruore'. Book v, lines 332–3.

Our own . . . mid-nineteenth century. The Penguin Dictionary of Historical Slang, ed. E. Partridge, abridged by T. Simpson (Harmondsworth, 1972), 831. Even so, it would be astonishing if the colloquialism were not in earlier use. Richard Luckett draws my attention to Pepys, ed. cit. i. 261: '. . . as if a man should shit in his hat and then clap it upon his head', which seems in the right vein.

Dryden's feelings about the general run of his worldly luck. Cf. McFadden, op. cit. 143: 'One of the most attractive traits in Dryden is his élan, his good spirits, and his lack of defensiveness; anxiety about his income is perhaps the only breach in his confident, cheerful approach to literature and the world. He probably was dissatisfied with himself for being so awkward at the game of success, for missing many opportunities that had been the making of several of his friends and dozens of his acquaintances.'

78 *Oldham himself . . . Argument'. The Poems of John Oldham*, 89. The punctuation of this transcript differs very slightly from that of the original text. Cf. *Some New Pieces Never Before Publisht*, by the Author of the *Satyrs upon the Jesuites* (London, 1681), 'Advertisement', a2ᵛ.

Robert Gould . . . verses. In Oldham, *Remains* (London, 1687).

Gould's tribute . . . 1687. Hammond, 208.

The Laureat . . . in print. E. H. Sloane, *Robert Gould: Seventeenth Century Satirist* (Philadelphia, 1940), 24, 121.

I concur with the view . . . cadence and rhyme. But whose view? If I had a reference for this it is now lost.

80 *Bunyan's . . . Mr Save-all.* John Bunyan, *The Pilgrim's Progress from this World to That which is to Come*, ed. J. B. Wharey, 2nd edn. by Roger Sharrock, corrected reprint (Oxford, 1967), 101.

Dryden anticipates Bunyan. But only in print. *The Pilgrim's Progress* was first published in the following year (1678). It is likely, however, that Bunyan had completed the work by 1672. See the edition by N. H. Keeble (Oxford, 1984), 264.

'my Lord Turn-about . . . Mr. Any-thing'. The Pilgrim's Progress, ed. Wharey and Sharrock, 99.

81 *Such absurdities . . . arbitrary.* Compare the placing of the expletive in Pound's 'Et Faim Saillir Les Loups des Boys', *Collected Early Poems of Ezra Pound* (London, 1977), 284.

'good sense, at all events'. Specimens of the Table Talk of the late Samuel Taylor Coleridge, 2 vols. (London, 1835), i. 123, 9 May 1830: 'Poetry is certainly something more than good sense, but it must be good sense, at all events, just as a palace is more than a house, but it must be a house, at least.'

'In the gloom . . . against it'. The Cantos of Ezra Pound, Fourth Collected edn. (London, 1987), 51.

Pound observed . . . ruins'. D. Anderson, 'Breaking the Silence: The Interview of Vanni Ronsisvalle and Pier Paolo Pasolini with Ezra Pound in 1968', *Paideuma*, 10 (1981), 331–45, at 336.

'Malice' . . . false'. Samuel Butler, *Prose Observations*, ed. H. de Quehen (Oxford, 1979), 60.

'running the difficult middle course'. Cf. S. N. Zwicker, *Politics and Language in Dryden's Poetry* (Princeton, 1984), esp. ch. 4, 'Politics and Religion: the "Middle Way" '.

5 'Envoi (1919)'

83 In 'Hugh Selwyn Mauberley' as it appears in *Personae: Collected Shorter Poems of Ezra Pound*, 'Envoi (1919)' is distinguished from the other poems of the sequence by being printed in italic type. This distinction was not made in the first edition issued in April 1920 by the Ovid Press. All eighteen poems are there printed in roman type, each with a decorative initial designed by Edward Wadsworth. In the table of contents of that volume 'Envoi 1919' is emphatically distinguished from the twelve poems of 'Part I' and the five of 'Part II'; it is printed in capitals, centred between two ruled lines. In the text, however, 'Envoi (1919)' is not set off in any way; there are no blank pages separating it from Parts I and II; no differentiation of typeface. One may reasonably hesitate to impute emblematic significance to typography or other details of book-production which may have been simple expediencies. Even so, in the years following the work's first appearance, 'Envoi (1919)', 'this lovely little poem' as Leavis called it (*New Bearings in English Poetry*, paperback edn. (Harmondsworth, 1963), 123), 'the masterpiece of the sequence' according to Pound's biographer Charles Norman (*Ezra Pound*, revised edn. (New York, 1969), 222), has many times been singled out for close and admiring attention.

It stands in opposition to (as some have said) or (as others have more recently argued) in apposition to 'Medallion', the eighteenth and final poem of the sequence. The earliest admirers of *Mauberley* established a way of looking at these two poems. 'Envoi (1919)' makes manifest the virtues of seventeenth-century English song, of the true voice of feeling matched by felicitous accuracy of diction and rhythm. 'Medallion' emanates from a more etiolated virtu, from principles and qualities in themselves preferable to the unprincipled and tasteless products of the market-place but vitiated by an atrophied aestheticism, an introverted refinement which is a lesser thing than felicitous accuracy declaring its intrinsic value 'in action'. This interpretation, culminating in 1955 with J. J. Espey's book-length study of the sequence (*Ezra Pound's 'Mauberley': A Study in Composition*, U.K. edn. (London, 1955)), was challenged by T. E. Connolly in his review of Espey's thesis ('Further Notes on Mauberley' *Accent*, 16/1 (Winter 1956), 59–67, at 60, 63). Unable to accept 'Envoi (1919)' as Pound's brilliant self-affirming, self-vindicating lyric of farewell to an England incapable of comprehending such beauty and such *virtù*, he assigned its authorship to 'H. S.

Mauberley', and this view of the poem's 'limitedness' was further emphasized by A. L. French in an essay published nine years later (' "Olympian Apathein": Pound's *Hugh Selwyn Mauberley* and Modern Poetry', *Essays in Criticism*, 15 (1965), 441); though the limitations were there claimed as Pound's not H. S. Mauberley's. That is to say: what Pound had proclaimed as his strength was rather to be seen as the outcome of a 'disabling' misjudgement. A third opinion, originating, in 1973, in an essay by J. Brantley Berryman (' "Medallion": Pound's Poem', *Paideuma*, 2 (1973), 391–8), is that 'Medallion', as much as 'Envoi (1919)', is to be understood as a successfully affirmative and definitive poem by Pound, unmodified by irony, and that each represents a particular mode which he had already described and advocated and which he is here putting into effect as forms having equal validity, equally opposed to the weak stridencies of English life and letters in the period immediately following the end of the First World War. 'Envoi (1919)' embodies the lyricism which Pound calls 'melopoeia' ('Marianne Moore and Mina Loy' (1918), in *Selected Prose*, 394), 'Medallion' displays the qualities of imagism or 'phanopoeia' (ibid. See the discussion by Berryman cited above. See also E. A. B. Jenner, ' "Medallion": Some Questions', *Paideuma*, 8 (1979), 153 ff.). The crucial challenge in each case is how to make momentary grace endure and indeed triumph over the vicissitudes of time and of mortal indifference or hostility.

'*To Thomas Campion . . . 1928*. *Literary Essays of Ezra Pound* (London, 1954), 155–7; H. Kenner, *The Pound Era*, paperback edn. (London, 1975), 393–4.

'*Chaque pièce . . . médaillon . . .*' Quoted by Berryman, *Paideuma*, 2 (1973), 397.

as Pound suggested . . . did not. *Literary Essays*, 285–9, at 285.

Among the English poets . . . neatness'. Ibid. 363, 368.

84 '*The eyes turn topaz.*' *Personae: Collected Shorter Poems of Ezra Pound* (London, 1952), 214.

'*interpretative crisis*'. Jenner, op. cit. 154.

'*strategic position*'. *Selected Prose*, 26.

'*the incessant . . . city*'. 'Gaudier–Brzeska Vortex', in *Gaudier–Brzeska: A Memoir*, by Ezra Pound, new edn. (Hessle, 1960), 24. See also Ezra Pound, *Guide to Kulchur*, 3rd impression (London, 1960), 67.

'*destroys . . . HSM*'. Jenner, op. cit. 156.

'*Part II . . . eye on*'. French, op. cit., 442.

'*Villon . . . fact*'. *The Spirit of Romance* (London, 1910), 187.

'lords . . . world'. Selected Prose, 160.

'sublimity . . . sense'. Literary Essays, 327.

'gross silence'. Impact: Essays on Ignorance and the Decline of American Civilization, ed. N. Stock (Chicago, 1960), 163.

85 *'Mauberley . . . novel'. The Letters of Ezra Pound 1907–1941,* ed. D. D. Paige (London, 1951), 248.

'étude in ephemera'. Literary Essays, 323.

'he does . . . all his own'. Ibid. 300.

'the domination . . . Henry James's style.' Ibid. 291.

'goes bail for the nation'. Patria Mia (Chicago, 1950), 64.

'catalogues . . . crudity'. Spirit of Romance, 163; *Selected Prose,* 115.

'disgusting . . . his own'. Pavannes and Divagations (Norfolk, Conn., 1958), 149.

'the most . . . opened'. Selected Prose, 373.

'shot himself . . . values.' Letters, 374; see also B. Knox, 'Allen Upward and Ezra Pound', *Paideuma,* 3 (1974), 71–83; A. D. Moody, 'Pound's Allen Upward', ibid. 4 (1975), 55–70.

'forced levity . . . spirit'. See Moody, *Paideuma,* 4 (1975), 63.

'the old combattant'. The Cantos of Ezra Pound, Fourth Collected Edition (London, 1987), 437.

86 *'you could call . . . respect him.' Impact,* 163.

'to free . . . affects'. Selected Prose, 330.

'Hoping . . . so'. The Complete Poems of Thomas Hardy, ed. J. Gibson (London, 1976), 468.

'This difference . . . commonplace.' Selected Prose, 41.

'capacious . . . observation'. Literary Essays, 311, 295.

'The passion . . . cry.' Ibid. 296.

87 *'In the gloom . . . against it.' Cantos,* ed. cit. 51.

'the αυάγκη . . . necessity'. Literary Essays, 300.

'the aimless . . . humanity'. Spirit of Romance, 124.

'the violent . . . wallow'. Ibid. 123–4.

'famous . . . arts'. C. F. Terrell, *A Companion to the Cantos of Ezra Pound,* 2 vols. (Berkeley, 1980, 1984), i. 37.

'. . . against . . . notch'. Guide to Kulchur, 159.

'templum aedificavit'. Canto 8: *Cantos,* ed. cit., 32.

'*The suicide . . . depression*'. *Cantos*, ed. cit. 625. See B. Knox, *Paideuma*, 3 (1974), 71–83.

'*nox . . . dies*'). See J. P. Sullivan, *Ezra Pound and Propertius: A Study in Creative Translation* (London, 1965), 142.

('When thou . . . vnder ground). *Campion's Works*, ed. P. Vivian (Oxford, 1909), 17, 358.

and Waller . . . rare'). *Poems, &c . . .* (London, 1645), 89–90:

> Goe lovely Rose,
> Tell her that wasts her time and mee,
> That now shee knowes,
> When I resemble her to thee,
> How sweet and fayr shee seems to bee . . .

The title-page states that 'All the Lyric Poems in this Booke were set by Mʳ HENRY LAVVES'.

88 '*Time . . . evil*'. *Cantos*, ed. cit. 147, 444.

'*Rhythm . . . TIME*'. *ABC of Reading*, 198, 202.

But . . . inscription. e.g.: 'Two kinds of banks have existed: The MONTE DEI PASCHI and the devils'; 'Our poetry and our prose have suffered incalculably whenever we have cut ourselves off from the French' (*Selected Prose*, 240, 354).

'*coercions* . . . *tyranny*'. Ibid. 159, 160.

'*anyone . . . middle.*' *Cantos*, 59.

('Law . . . pivot'. *Cantos*, 269; see R. Schultz, 'A Detailed Chronology of Ezra Pound's London Years, 1908–1920. Part One . . .', *Paideuma*, 11 (1982), 456–72, at 466.

'*Kung . . . meaning . . .*'). *Guide to Kulchur*, 18.

'*life-long . . . passion*'. *Selected Prose*, 159.

'*prominent . . . discard*'. Ibid. 408, 431.

'*Provincialism . . . uniformity*'. Ibid. 160.

'*a soft . . . verbiage*'. *Literary Essays*, 185; *Guide to Kulchur*, 324.

89 '*the preciseness . . . precise*'. *Spirit of Romance*, 92, 93.

'*substance . . . light*'. Ibid. 160. In *A Drunk Man Looks at the Thistle* (1926), Hugh MacDiarmid, who, despite extreme political differences, admired Pound and described himself as being 'in some ways greatly influenced by' him, was drawn to these same lines by Dante. See *The Complete Poems of Hugh MacDiarmid*, ed. M. Grieve and W. R. Aitken, 2 vols. (Harmondsworth, 1985), i. 153–4; Hugh MacDiarmid, *The Company I've Kept: Essays in Autobiography* (London, 1966), 170.

'*The style . . . revelation.*' *Patria Mia*, 42.

'*new . . . triumphant*'. Ibid. 48–9.

'*pianola*' *. . . yacht*'. *Personae*, ed. cit. 198, 203.

'*courteous . . . old*'. *Patria Mia*. 49.

'*The traditional . . . seem*'. *Selected Prose*, 331.

'*derivative convention*'. See D. Anderson, 'A Language to Translate Into: The Pre-Elizabethan Idiom of Pound's Later Cavalcanti Translations', *Studies in Medievalism* (Akron, Ohio), 2/1 (Fall 1982), 10.

90 *born out of their due time.* Cf. *Spirit of Romance*, 99: 'Both Dante and Shakespear were men "born in their due time" '; *Selected Prose*, 26: 'To be born a troubadour in Provence in the twelfth century was to be born, you would say, "in one's due time".'

a genus . . . aligned himself. As—arguably—did T. S. Eliot. See 'Baudelaire in our Time', in *For Lancelot Andrewes* (London, 1928), 86– 99, esp. 97: 'The important fact about Baudelaire is that he was essentially a Christian, born out of his due time, and a classicist, born out of his due time.' See also Thomas Hardy, 'In Tenebris II': 'Till I think I am one born out of due time, who has no calling here' (*The Variorum Edition of the Complete Poems of Thomas Hardy*, ed. J. Gibson (London, 1979), 168). The allusion is to 1 Corinthians, 15: 8, in the Version of 1611: 'And last of all he was seene of me also, as of †one borne out of due time [†*or, an abortiue.*'

'*The English . . . days.*' *Personae*, ed. cit. 201. See T. E. Connolly, 'Further Notes on Mauberley', *Accent*, 16/1: 63.

'*motz el son*'. *Selected Prose*, 37; *Literary Essays*, 170.

practised for the last time in England by Campion and Lawes. Cf. 'Even the deified Purcell is not up to Lawes' (First Book of Ayres, especially) in these matters': *Ezra Pound and Music: The Complete Criticism*, ed. R. M. Schafer (London, 1978), 104 (30 May 1918).

'*hardness*' *and* '*logopoeia*' *Literary Essays*, 285, 33.

'*Envoi (1919)*' *. . . the book will have.* E. Hesse's 'Books Behind the Cantos (Part 1)', *Paideuma*, 1: 138–51, bears on this.

'*you use . . . irony.*' 'Ezra Pound, Letters to Natalie Barney', ed. R. Sieburth, *Paideuma*, 5 (1976), 279–295, at 282.

the '*not quite it*' *and the* '*not quite not it*'. *Selected Prose*, 31.

'*the one adjective . . . Murano*'. *Pavannes and Divagations*, 5–6.

91 *Madison Cawein.* See *Poetry: A Magazine of Verse*, 1/4 (Jan. 1913), 104–5.

Arthur Upson. See *The Collected Poems of Arthur Upson*, 2 vols. (Minneapolis, 1909), ii. 168, 166.

The first . . . Verse. See *The Little Book of Modern Verse*, ed. Jessie B. Rittenhouse (New York, 1913), 181–2.

Pound . . . tributes to his work . . . 1917. *Literary Essays*, 431–40. See D. Gallup, *A Bibliography of Ezra Pound* (London, 1969), 210, 217, 218.

'mak[ing] it new'. See e.g. *Make It New: Essays by Ezra Pound* (London, 1934): design on title-page; *Cantos*, 265; W. Cookson, *A Guide to the Cantos of Ezra Pound* (London, 1985), 59; Terrell, *Companion*, i. 205.

'once been . . . democracy'. *Literary Essays*, 436.

'the vortex of pattern'. Ibid. 434.

'impressionist . . . music'. Ibid.

'This old music . . . concentration.' Ibid. 433.

('Out of the conquered Past . . . Death'). *The Little Book of Modern Verse*, 20th impression (March 1923), 181.

92 *'constant affinity . . . Lovelace.'* *The Younger American Poets*, by Jessie B. Rittenhouse (1904; repr. Freeport, NY, 1968), 29, 35.

'at my grates no Althea'. *Cantos*, 519.

'olde . . . writers'. *Literary Essays*, 395; cf. Gallup, 253 (c727).

'the "sweet . . . tone'. *Literary Essays*, 323.

'worn smooth . . . singing'. *Guide to Kulchur*, 281.

'you cannot call . . . upon him'. *Patria Mia*, 31.

93 *those claims . . . poetry*. E.g. 'All values ultimately come from our judicial sentences' (*Letters*, 249); 'The tyro can not play about with such things, the game is too dangerous' (*Literary Essays*, 283).

'By what . . . beauty.' *Selected Prose*, 47.

'An Anachronism . . . knowledge'. *Pavannes and Divagations*, 89–90.

'the naivest . . . sense'. Ibid. 8.

'Till change . . . alone'. *Personae*, ed. cit. 207.

'What thou . . . from thee'. *Cantos*, 521.

'Beauty . . . another'. *Literary Essays*, 241.

'Beauty . . . accusation'. *Selected Prose*, 116.

' "beauty . . . Beardsley'. *Cantos*, 444.

of 'conflicts . . . passéism'. Pound/Joyce: The Letters of Ezra Pound to James Joyce, with Pound's Essays on Joyce, ed. F. Reed (London, 1968), 113 (editorial commentary).

the 'archaizing . . . collections'. D. Davie, 'The Universe of Ezra Pound', *Paideuma*, 1 (1972), 263–9, at 268.

94 *'mellifluous archaism'. Pound/Joyce*, 122.

'sheer poetic . . . poetry'. Spirit of Romance, 150, 160, 234.

'tones clear as brown amber'. Literary Essays, 433.

parochial. Patria Mia, 64: '. . . being born an American is no excuse for being content with a parrochial standard.'

'the beautiful' . . . τὸ καλόν . See J. Espey, 'The Inheritance of τὸ καλόν ', in *New Approaches to Ezra Pound*, ed. E. Hesse (London, 1969), 319–30. See Patrides's commentary on Masson's translation of Milton's letter to Charles Diodati (23 Sept. 1637): 'The Latin original provides here a Greek phrase which specifies "the beautiful" as τὸ καλόν , which Milton realized implies both an aesthetic and a moral judgement' (Milton, *Selected Prose*, ed. cit. 361).

when reading Coleridge. Espey, op. cit. 319.

'We see . . . market place'. Personae, ed. cit. 199.

a letter of William James. The Letters of William James, Edited by his Son, 2 vols. (London, 1920), ii. 117.

a brusque note to . . . Elkin Mathews. Pound/Joyce, 286; dated 2 June/July (?) 19(??). Mathews feared that a prosecution might be brought against certain poems in *Lustra*.

'quicksand . . . concealers . . .' Impact, 163.

95 *('pli selon pli'). Cantos*, 15; *Companion to the Cantos*, i. 13 n. 21.

'a vortex . . . odds.' Selected Prose, 386.

'Prince . . . Conteurs'. See R. Sieburth, in *Paideuma*, 5 (1975), 280.

'the great . . . benignity'. Literary Essays, 322, 295.

'collage . . . misreadings'. H. Kenner, *The Poetry of Ezra Pound* (London, 1951), 151.

'bravura' . . . powers'. OED, ed. cit. ii. 498.

'Can a man . . . Beddoes has done so'. Selected Prose, 351.

96 *'beauty of the means'.* Ibid. 41.

'Labour . . . very slowly.' Pavannes and Divagations, 219–20.

Pound also . . . ever since'. Letters, 340; Kenner, *The Pound Era*, 330. See also *The Cantos of Ezra Pound*, ed. cit. 572 (Canto 87). See also the commentary in Terrell, *A Companion to the Cantos*, i. 198–9: 'As opposed to art, where "Slowness is beauty" . . . usurers are in a hurry: "Time is money!".'

'strongly marked time'. Yeats to Lady Gregory, 10 Dec. 1909 (*The Letters of W. B. Yeats*, ed. A. Wade (London, 1954), 543).

'He reads it . . . majestical'. A. Ginsberg, 'Allen Verbatim', *Paideuma*, 3 (1974), 253–73, at 263.

'Rhythm . . . very slow'. D. Gordon, ' "Root/Br./By Product" in Pound's Confucian Ode 166', *Paideuma*, 3 (1970), 13–32, at 25.

Pound's theory . . . frequencies.' Guide to Kulchur, 73.

Pound reads . . . anything else. See R. M. Schafer, 'The Developing Theories of Absolute Rhythm and Great Bass', *Paideuma*, 2 (1973), 23–35: 'Hugh Kenner has suggested that the term *absolute rhythm* may have been stimulated by Rémy de Gourmont's *Le Latin mystique* (Paris, 1892). Although the precise expression does not appear there, the idea may indeed have been suggested by certain remarks in that book . . .' (25).

delli occhi . . . tardi e gravi'. Dante's Purgatorio with a Translation into English Triple Rhyme by Laurence Binyon (London, 1938), 66–7; *Dante's Inferno with a Translation into English Triple Rhyme* by Laurence Binyon (London, 1933), 44–5. See also *Spirit of Romance*, 118. See also 'I Vecchii' ('Mœurs Contemporains', VII) and Canto 7 (*Personae*, ed. cit. 192; *Cantos*, ed. cit. 24).

97 *'The massive head . . . incision'.* Literary Essays, 295.

that 'quality . . . things'. D. Gordon with C. F. Terrell, 'Meeting E. P. and then . . .' *Paideuma*, 3 (1974), 343–60, at 351.

'inevitable . . . field'. Guide to Kulchur, 105–6. Pound thought he saw such qualities in Mussolini! Here as elsewhere one clings grimly to the sense of his own dictum: 'you could call [him] a damn fool *and* respect him' (*Impact*, 163).

'I wrote . . . twenty-five years.' Quoted by B. Knox in *Paideuma*, 3 (1974), 79.

('prose kinema'). Personae, ed. cit. 198.

'Professionals . . . taken out . . .' Pound/Joyce, 51.

'full . . . unswerving'. Gaudier–Brzeska, ed. cit. 99. Pound says that these 'are the sort of phrases that arise in the literary mind in the presence of Epstein's sculpture'. Pound claims, on the following page, that 'there are two types of mind which the mediocre world hates most'. One is 'this mind of the slow gestation, whose absoluteness terrifies "the man in the street" '. The other 'follows the lightning for model'.

the 1939 disc . . . *'Envoi (1919)'*. For information on Pound's several recordings see Gallup, op. cit. 390–2.

98 *'perhaps . . . imperfections'*. *Literary Essays*, 442.

'consummation of métier'. Ibid. 170.

'melody . . . the soul'. Ibid. 442.

' "absolute . . . expressed'. Ibid. 9. See also *Gaudier–Brzeska*, ed. cit. 84: 'I said in the preface to my *Guido Cavalcanti* that I believed in an absolute rhythm . . .' What he actually wrote in that introduction was: 'When we know more of overtones we will see that the tempo of every masterpiece is absolute, and is exactly set by some further law of rhythmic accord.' See Schafer, loc. cit.

99 *'On his one and only visit'*. Jessie B. Rittenhouse, *My House of Life: An Autobiography* (Boston and New York, 1934), 228–9. Miss Rittenhouse recalls that 'he was about to sail for England, being unable longer to "bear the brunt of America" '. This would date the meeting as very early in 1911. See R. Schultz, 'A Detailed Chronology . . .' *Paideuma*, 11 (1982), 461.

Though she found . . . the Rittenhouse ethos. Miss Rittenhouse's review appeared on pages 575–8 of *The Bookman: A Magazine of Literature and Life*, 46/5 (Jan. 1918). Her review also contained appraisals of *The Chinese Nightingale* by Vachel Lindsay and *Asphalt*, by Orrick Johns. My attention was drawn to this review by V. Mondolfo, 'An Annotated Bibliography of Criticism of Ezra Pound 1918–1924', *Paideuma*, 5 (1975), 303–22, at 304.

'charm . . . thing'. From Miss Rittenhouse's comments on Orrick Johns, loc. cit.

('See, they return . . . Wavering!'). *Collected Early Poems* (London, 1977), 198.

100 *'reflective' . . . feel of the thing'*. See S. M. Gall, 'Pound and the Modern Melic Tradition: Towards a Demystification of "Absolute Rhythm" ', *Paideuma*, 8 (1979), 35–45, at 37.

'The Coming of War: Actaeon'. *Personae*, ed. cit. 117.

'To break . . . heave'. *Cantos*, 518.

the nine . . . disguise. H. Witemeyer, *The Poetry of Ezra Pound: Forms and Renewal: 1908–1920* (Berkeley and Los Angeles, 1969), 193.

'detail . . . justice'. *Letters*, 366.

('Wrong . . . acorn'). *Personae*, ed. cit. 97.

poetry . . . music.' *Selected Prose*, 394.

'*good verbalism*' . . . "*usage*" '. *Literary Essays*, 283; *ABC of Reading*, 37.

101 '*the utterance . . . despair*'. *Selected Prose*, 394.

Versions . . . '*Contemporiana*'. Loc. cit.

'*done cantos . . . done about it*'. *Pound/Joyce*, 163.

'*canorous lyric measures*'. Leavis's phrase, in *New Bearings in English Poetry*, 122–3.

'*a dance . . . characters*'. *Selected Prose*, 394; the 1918 definition. Compare and contrast Pound's subsequent definition, where 'intellect' replaces 'intelligence'. See *Literary Essays*, 25.

'*When Pound . . . Generation*'. See W. B. Yeats, *Autobiographies* (London, 1955).

'*I said . . . difficult,*",' Ibid. 333.

'*noble courage*'. W. B. Yeats, *Memoirs*, ed. D. Donoghue (London, 1972), 92.

'*spirit of mockery*'. *Autobiographies*, 333.

INDEX

Index